METALLICA™
UNBOUND

The Unofficial Biography

BY K.J. Doughton

WARNER BOOKS

A Time Warner Company

*An MCP, Inc. production
for Warner Books, Inc.*

Design
Lorinda Sullivan

Photography
Unless otherwise
indicated, photographs
are © Ross Halfin.

Illustration
© Brian Schroder

™ The Metallica name and logo are trademarks of Metallica.

Use of the Metallica logo is not an indication of the endorsement by Metallica of this book.

Grateful acknowledgment is given for the use of portions of the following songs: "Fade to Black" by James Hetfield, Lars Ulrich, Cliff Burton and Kirk Hammett © 1984 Creeping Death Music (ASCAP). "One" by James Hetfield and Lars Ulrich © 1988 Creeping Death Music (ASCAP). "Dyers Eve" by James Hetfield, Lars Ulrich and Kirk Hammett © Creeping Death Music (ASCAP)

Warner Books, Inc.
1271 Avenue of the Americas,
New York, NY 10020

Ⓦ A Time Warner Company

Photo Credits
Photos on pages p. 48 (bottom) © Richard Brackett; p. 96 © Jaye Clarke; p. 21 © Colleen Copeland; p. 49 © Kathleen Cuevas; p. 88 © K.J. Doughton; pp. 57, 58, 63 © Eric De Haas; pp. 30, 35, 37, 41, 42, 46, 47, 48 (top), 120, 123, 124, 125, 132, 138 © Brian Lew; p. 44, 126, 146 © Brian Markham; p. 19 © David Marrs; p. 153 © Mike Meals; pp. 38, 45, 53, 54, 62, 66, 67, 69, 70, 74, 75, 77, 90, 122, 141, 144, 145, 147, 151 © Harald Oimeon; pp. 11, 143, 152 © Ron Quintana; pp. 23, 28 © Patrick Scott; p. 135 © Wayne Vanderkuil; pp. 169, 170, 171 © Mike Wasco.

Cover design by Diane Luger
Cover hand lettering by Carl Dellacroce
Cover photo by Ross Halfin
Cover illustration by Brian Schroder

Printed in the United States
of America
First Printing: August 1993
10 9 8 7 6 5 4 3 2 1

Library of Congress Cataloging-in-Publication Data

Doughton, K.J.
Metallica Unbound / K.J. Doughton.
p. cm.
Discography: p
ISBN 0-446-39486-6 (pbk)
1. Metallica (Musical group) 2. Rock Musicians—
United States—Biography. I. Title
ML421.M48D7 1993
782.42166'092'2—dc20
[B]   92-21192
                                        CIP
                                        MN

Acknowledgments

This book is the end result of a heavy metal camaraderie that has existed over the past 10 years between several particularly active tape traders, fanzine writers, photographers, roadies, musicians, bootleggers, record label executives, managers, and promoters, all of whom played some part in Metallica's exciting, decade-long climb to spectacular heights. *Metallica Unbound* would not have been possible without these generous resources.

Extra special thanks to Bill Stephen and MCP, Inc., and Anne Douglas Milburn at Warner Books for making all of this happen. Eternal gratitude to Brian ("Umlaut") Lew, Ron ("Spon Q.") Quintana, and Harald ("O") Oimoen for their invaluable editorial assistance, stories, photos, and memorabilia. Special thanks to "interviewees" James Hetfield, Lars Ulrich, Kirk Hammett, Jason Newsted, John Marshall, Brian Slagel, Patrick Scott, Dave Marrs, Sheila Marrs, Dave Mustaine, Bob Nalbandian, John Bush, Joey Vera, and Duke Erickson for their time, insight, and information. Hats off to Cliff Burnstein, Peter Mensch, Linda Walker, Ian Jeffrey, Metallica's tour manager, and the entire Q-Prime management team for providing access to the band and offering their support and friendship.

Much appreciation to Ross Halfin for allowing me to peruse his incredible collection of photographs and to use a few of them in the following pages. Thanks also to Jacqui Lugo for her photo-selecting assistance. Many thanks to Lorinda Sullivan for her hours of layout and design work, Brad Tolinski and *Guitar World* for setting things into motion, and Pushead for his twisted, one-of-a-kind artwork.

Additional thanks to Mark DeVito, Mike Barnett, Greg Kerr, Eric DeHaas, Andre Verhuysen, Mike Wasco, Mike Meals, Jan Burton, and Ian Kallen.

Family apologies department: To my wife Patricia, for tolerating my many selfish days and nights of obsessive word-processing, going for *The Guinness Book of Records'* "Highest Monthly Phone Bill" record by means of rambling long-distance conversations to New York and Holland, spending our last red cent on unnecessary import CDs, trivial music items, and other such forms of senseless neglect. To my parents, for their unflinching support of my off-kilter, unusual, financially suicidal hobbies and obsessions.

Extreme contrasts department: This book is dedicated to Metallica for 10 years of relentless, uncompromising music-making, to the underground fans who made the Eighties a vital and exciting time for music, and to Corinne Doughton, my beloved new daughter (welcome to the world, little one).

CONTENTS

GARAGE DAYS

MY ASSOCIATION WITH Metallica began when a friend received the group's first four-song demo tape in 1982. Lantz Shapiro, the other headbanger trapped in the dilapidated Oregon mill town of Roseburg, scored the tape in a trade with drummer Lars Ulrich's right-hand demo distributor, Patrick Scott. Like myself, Shapiro was a detached, shy high school student whose idea of fun was cuddling up at home with his Stratocaster and playing air-guitar to the heaviest metal the musical spirits could dish out.

Contemptuous of the passé Ted Nugent and Styx selections that filled the record bins of southern Oregon, Lantz and I took weekend drives to Eugene and Portland with money earned from after-school dishwashing stints at the local Denny's restaurant, and blew it on metal-filled scriptures like England's *Kerrang!* magazine and European import albums like Venom's *Welcome to Hell* and Accept's *Restless and Wild*.

We hiked up the phone bill at Roseburg High School by making long-distance calls to Northwest bands like Crysys and the Wild Dogs, and to such renowned authorities as Mike Varney and Johnny Zazula, two independent metal record label owners who cast high-profile shadows

Opposite: Metallica, 1991

over the underground scene. Our school's journalism department, confronted with a $400 phone bill one month, caught on and forced us to reimburse them for the costly correspondence.

We didn't care. Such antics were prompted by the same unexplainable allegiance to metal music that had seen Lars Ulrich, an alienated Danish kid in Los Angeles, work so relentlessly to carve out his own unlikely niche. The dark energy of metal music appeared as a seductive outroad from that island of discontent on which most teens in the early Eighties felt stranded–where one's hometown seemed like a stifling armpit of civilization. We hated Roseburg's woodsy confines as much as Lars hated Los Angeles.

Then the Metallica demo package arrived. We were devastated by the music's distinctly un-American combination of frantic riffing with a blazing pace. This was like nothing we'd ever heard. As noise addicts pioneering new audio frontiers, we felt we were onto something different with Metallica; it was time to track the group down and learn more.

An early concert flyer for The Concert Factory.

"Fuck, man! You're kidding," exclaimed Lars from the other end of a phone, amazed at the notion that someone stuck in such an unlikely state as Oregon would have his band's tape. The drummer's pleased profanity marked the dawn of yet another friendship forged in metal.

Lars assigned me to run Metallica's fan club; my job was to help spread the word of what I knew would be the next great metal band. I duped hundreds of demos and sent them to every pen pal, fanzine, and indie label within range of a postmarked envelope. Brian Lew, a Y&T fanatic from Sunnyvale, California, who had been immersing himself in the tide of new metal sounds, flipped out over the Metallica pilot demo project and became the band's Bay Area cheerleader. Lew, myself, and others pushed out tapes in the manner of ruthless drug lords working to satisfy addicted masses. By the time the band pulled into the San Francisco Stone in September of '82, Metallica had already secured a groundswell of fans.

I originally ran the Metallica fan club from the basement of my parents' home. Lars would send me handwritten newsletters and dictate band information over the phone, with which I would formulate printed newsletters to send to all inquirers, along with the latest T-shirts, demos, and pins. Eventually, however, the huge mail pull (nearly 300 letters a week by the time *Master of Puppets* was released) was too much for a rural Northwest okie to keep up with, so the fan club was surrendered to an East Coast merchandising company.

I'll never forget receiving those initial quirky prized parcels from my high-strung, unusually motivated Danish buddy. In his letters, he coupled exceptional drive and intensity with a distinct, self-kidding humor. Along with a copy of the band's four-song pre-*Ride the Lightning* demo, for instance, he included an ominous warning: "Just remember that the tape was done in one (1, uno, ein, en) take and is full of *fuck-ups*, but as they say, so what? And remember, you are the only one outside of band members with a tape, so if we find it floating around, we will send the Hit Squad!!! Don't even *tell* anyone!!"

Since then, the Metallica saga has, as they say, become history. Major label backing and corporate management muscle pushed the band above and beyond the underground threshold and into the commercial limelight, leading to record sales beyond the 10 million unit mark. The band is now regarded as the Led Zeppelin of the Eighties and Nineties, and they show no signs of having peaked. Despite this high visibility, Metallica have never shed their punkish, cultlike, "against-the-grain" skin, a vibe retained from those glorious early days when word-of-mouth, high-octane club shows, and a fistful of demos were the only methods of exposure they had.

Metallica at El Cerrito Metallipad, 1983.

This book was written as a way of putting the Metallica story into a well-deserved time capsule, emphasizing the band's "underground" days with exclusive photos and memorabilia that have never before been published. Most of the information was graciously supplied by friends, fans, and associates of the band, and will appear alongside chapters on the Metallica history, an interview with band co-founder James Hetfield, a section of fans' written memories and perspectives, and a rundown of all Metallica products in existence, from records to promo items and merchandise.

I hope that *Metallica Unbound* serves as a worthy reference guide for Metallibangers, Metal Militants, Metallicatz, Metallithrashers, Metalliragers, and Metallifreaks worldwide: the most loyal, dedicated and fanatical fans of any band alive. This book is dedicated to all of you, and to the only band that deserves you...Metallica.

L.A. ROOTS

CHAPTER 1

ONE WINTRY EVENING in 1973, Deep Purple roared through a concert performance in Copenhagen, Denmark. Sitting in the crowded auditorium, a bit to his own surprise, was a Danish tennis pro named Torben Ulrich, accompanied by his nine-year-old son, Lars. The elder Ulrich was somewhat out of his element. An enigmatic figure, he was entrenched in the rigorous disciplines of professional tennis; on the other hand, he was also immersed in Europe's jazz underground scene. In fact, Torben dubbed legendary saxophonist Dexter Gordon godfather to Lars. His devotion to jazz went far beyond that of the ordinary fan–the music seemed to serve as a therapeutic release for the father, whose self-styled, nonconformist appearance would be summed up by his son years later as that of a "hippie-freak tennis player."

It wasn't until Torben traded his penchant for small, smoky clubs for the confines of a crowded auditorium that Lars would be introduced to the music that would become his passion. Friends of the elder Ulrich passed along extra tickets to the Deep Purple concert. The spectacle of Ritchie Blackmore acrobatically abusing his Strat opened Lars's eyes to the bombast and energy of the heavy rock scene, and the next day he went record shopping and scored his first album, a copy of *Fireball*. At 13, he persuaded his grandmother to buy him a primitive drumkit, which he enthusiastically pounded in

Opposite: James onstage, 1989

a room filled with wall-poster images of Deep Purple and Kiss.

Although toms and sticks were taking precedence over nets and racquets in their boy's life, the Ulrich family migrated from Denmark to Newport Beach, California, in August of 1980 in the hope that Lars would find the sunny climate more conducive to tennis. Soon afterwards, however, destiny would intervene and take the young Dane on a musical roller coaster ride.

☧

The town of Downey sits like a small piece in the middle of a very large L.A. puzzle. Driving down its main drag, Firestone Boulevard, one gets the sense of a delicate, traditional community being crushed on all sides by a maze of industrial factories and impoverished neighborhoods. Claustrophobia comes easily in Downey, and so does boredom.

In the late Seventies, a sleepy-eyed student at Downey East Middle School named James Hetfield seized upon music to counter the pent-up vibes that suffocated his town. Dave Marrs, Hetfield's friend and fellow music aficionado, recalls the heavy metal listening sessions the two held in the ninth grade. "I remember us taking a biology class together," said Marrs. "I had my Kiss T-shirt on, and he was a big Aerosmith fan, and we began talking about bands. That's when we started hitting it off, playing records, and really getting into metal."

Over the course of the next three years, James traveled a bumpy road—his mother died of cancer, an experience James would later

Above: James Hetfield, beginning his metalmorphosis at Downey High School. Opposite: Performing onstage a decade later.

incorporate into the song "The God That Failed." As Christian Scientists, James's parents shunned medical treatment and their son was forbidden to attend health classes, a circumstance he resented deeply. Soon after his mother died, James relocated to La Brea, where he lived with his brother-in-law. "That whole situation hurt James a lot," remembers Marrs, somberly.

Hetfield immersed himself in music, using rock 'n roll as an escape from the painful realities around him. Prior to moving to Brea, for instance, James had played guitar in his first band, Obsession, formed by a trio of his Downey High buddies, including brothers Rich and Ron Veloz (drums and bass, respectively), and second guitarist Jim Arnold. "At the time," recalls Hetfield, "the band had no singer. We jammed in the garage every afternoon, doing covers of Thin Lizzy and Black Sabbath, the heavier stuff. We played two or three parties. But after my mom died I had to live with my brother-in-law and go to school in Brea. But I'd drive back and play with them on the weekends."

The Obsession project gave way as Hetfield found a new crop of noisemakers at Brea High. James recalls holding lunchtime jams with a guitarist remembered only as Troy, whose musical tastes were driven by Neil Young-style acoustics, and drummer Jim Mulligan. Like Hetfield, Mulligan was into Rush and it was only a matter of time before Troy was left out of their raucous noontime sessions. "Troy kinda freaked out 'cause we were playing stuff with volume and pounding drums, his acoustics couldn't keep up. I burned a bridge, but I'd met Mulligan."

Soon afterwards, during a woodshop class, James eyed a classmate lugging around part of a Flying V guitar. And so he met Hugh Tanner, and the two aspiring axemen began jamming. With the Neil Peart-obsessed skinbeater Mulligan in one corner, and Tanner in the other, James formed Phantom Lord, and sang and played second guitar. Bassists would come and go.

After graduation, James went back to Downey, when an old friend named Ron McGovney offered to house him. "Most of my friends were hanging there," James explains. "Ron's mom owned four houses stacked behind each other. So there was a vacant house I got to live in. There were no expenses, except maybe buying my own food. I was pretty lucky."

The improved living quarters also doubled as a rehearsal space, and with McGovney learning bass, the scene was set for the breakup of Phantom Lord and the creation of Leather Charm. Mulligan and Tanner continued their familiar posts, McGovney was broken in as bassist, and James sang. But the lineup didn't gel;

although the band remained afloat, it was destined for trouble.

✠

As Leather Charm was trying to break out of mediocrity, Lars Ulrich, much like Hetfield, was turning to music as an escape–in his case, from the cultural isolation of Newport Beach. The fourteen-year-old's racket-swinging halted somewhat when the court-hopper found competition a bit fierce. His confidence dwindling, Lars abandoned tennis to hunt down metal records.

Ulrich wasn't alone in his passion. The New Wave Of British Heavy Metal (NWOBHM) belched forth UK bands like Iron Maiden, Def Leppard, Saxon, Trespass, Diamond Head, Sweet Savage, Angel Witch, Venom, Sledgehammer, Raven, and Holocaust. The British bands developed a strong following among American kids who were fed up with the limitations of an empty U.S. hard-rock scene and eager to sample the new musical merchandise from overseas.

Farther north, a burly college student and Sears employee named Brian Slagel, another reknowned vinyl bloodhound on the scent of rare metal LPs and singles, would eventually start Metal Blade Records. But back then, Slagel remembers hooking up with Lars and metalhead John Kornarens on record-buying romps.

"Lars was a little bit younger," stated Slagel. "He was about 16, and we were both 18. We would drive up to a record store, and he would be in the store, and into the metal section before we had even opened the car doors."

Slagel remembers visiting Lars shortly after the metal-crazed Dane had bought a drum set. "We were listening to a bunch of stuff and he had the set sitting unassembled in a corner. Lars pointed to it, with a twinkle in his eye, and said, 'I'm gonna start a band with that.' But I didn't take him seriously."

✠

In April, history was forged when Hetfield and Tanner agreed to meet the fledgling skinbeater in an Irvine rehearsal room to jam. Caught without a drummer, they called on Lars to audition.

"Hugh got that jam together," recalls James. "I don't remember exactly how it came about. Lars wasn't that good back then. So we kinda said, 'We'll call you some other time.' But we never did."

It wouldn't be long, however, before the two would meet again.

✠

Determined to improve his trapset skills, Lars enrolled at West Coast Drums, bought a second-hand Camco kit, and jammed with other musicians. But Ulrich's Euro-British sensibilities clashed with the lame posturing prevalent among L.A.'s flaky population

Ad promoting Metal Massacre compilation album, 1982.

of amateur rock musicians.

Fed up, Lars flew to England at the conclusion of the school year. The day he arrived, Diamond Head played a gig in London. After watching the show, he prowled the venue eager for a chance to meet the band. Collaring Sean Harris, the Zeppelinesque group's singer, Lars introduced himself. Harris instantly recalled the letters Lars had written the band and invited him to stay at his parent's Stourbridge home to hang with Diamond Head for two months.

Patrick Scott explains his Dutch friend's insatiable appetite for Diamond Head's slick blend of impassioned, melodic vocals and crunchy guitar riffs: "Lars felt the Diamond Head songs were really epic, with these huge middle parts and giant riffs. He felt they'd be the new Led Zeppelin."

After two months of observing the group's operation, Lars grew determined to get his own thing going in the States. He returned to Huntington Beach in November, musically invigorated and full of new ideas.

✠

Meanwhile, back in Topanga Canyon, Brian Slagel had acquired a reputation as L.A.'s "Mister Metal." He'd ditched his job in favor of Oz Records and launched the fanzine *New Heavy Metal Revue*. Underground metal was becoming the rage, and he capitalized on his positions to promote new bands. His ever-growing influence was demonstrated when Motley Crue became rock-media darlings after Slagel collaborated with rock journalist Sylvie Simmons on a "Los Angeles Heavy Metal" spread in *Sounds*.

Slagel figured the best way to expand his metal network was to form a record label. Indie imprints specializing in metal were sprouting like mushrooms after a hard rain: British labels like Neat, Heavy Metal Records, Ebony Records, and Bronze were familiar to NWOBHM collectors, and a Bay Area guitar fanatic, Mike Varney, had gotten America into the picture with his label, Shrapnel. Slagel jumped into the Indie race with Metal Blade Records, announcing his first release to be a compilation of L.A. metal bands entitled *Metal Massacre*.

Just as Varney created Shrapnel to give hot, unknown guitarists widespread exposure on a series of U.S. Metal showcase collections, Slagel's idea in producing *Metal Massacre* was to jump-start the careers of bands in his areas. Word of the project reached Newport Beach, where Lars immediately made it a priority to assemble a band and get onto the record.

✠

Despite their disastrous first meeting, Lars called James again, this time as a musical rebel with a cause, and convinced him to team up. "Lars kept in touch with James," says Marrs, "because James was the only one he knew who was into heavy stuff. He didn't know as much as Lars did about obscure stuff, but he liked Aerosmith, Sabbath, stuff like that. I think that even back then, Lars saw something in James that he wanted, so he kept on bothering him."

After being offered the chance to compose and play a song on Slagel's upcoming record, Hetfield invited the drummer to the McGovney family practice pad. At the time, Leather Charm had disbanded and James welcomed fresh musical camaraderie. When Lars arrived, the two realized that in order to immortalize themselves on the *Metal Massacre* disc, they'd need three things: a song, a group name, and a functioning band. To accomplish the first, they dusted off a Leather Charm number called "Hit the Lights." Meanwhile, Lars stole the name Metallica from a fanzine editor in the Bay Area named Ron Quintana. As the story goes, Quintana had invited him to help decide on a name for his soon-to-be published heavy metal fanzine. When they narrowed down the monikers to Metallica and Metal Mania, Lars assured Quintana that Metal Mania was the one. Meanwhile, he adopted Metallica!

For the group, Lars and James auditioned several musicians, but were unimpressed with the L.A. candidates. "There were loads of people," sighs James. "No one really had the stuff, though. They

Kirk in New York, 1983.

weren't aggressive! It was annoying. I was always comparing people to myself. I thought, well, if he ain't better than me, he ain't gonna be in the band. I'll just play the guitar, too."

Meanwhile, McGovney had been invited to join as bassist, but he was indifferent. "Ron wasn't interested," confirms James. "He was just kinda there."

Under these circumstances, they realized they were failing miserably, and a finished product was needed quickly. However, since they'd be recording "Hit the Lights" on a four-track, they reasoned that a complete group wasn't necessary. Hetfield wagered he could play and record the bass, guitar, and vocal tracks separately, while Ulrich played drums. The only department they weren't prepared to fill was lead guitar. Enter Dave Mustaine.

Mustaine was a brash, blond axeman who'd recently left Panic and was hungry for a new gig. He got one after calling Lars and ranting through an eager sales pitch that would seal his reputation as the band's motormouth. At the time of his recruitment, Lars and James had already mixed the other tracks—his job was merely to play a lead break.

Although Mustaine rose to the occasion, Lars and James decided, with only hours to go before the "Hit the Lights" demo was due for submission, that a second lead by a different guitarist would be essential! Lars knew a Jamaican guitarist named Lloyd Grant who was available. So, on the way to Hollywood's Bijou Studio, where Slagel was already finished mixing the other *Metal Massacre* tracks, the band screeched into Grant's driveway, lugged the four-track into his front room, and watched him churn a second lead break. The "Hit the Lights" recipe was now complete.

"I remember we had this four-track recorder," explains Hetfield, recalling the last-minute struggle. "It had tracks for drums, bass, guitar, and vocals. Because there were no vocals in certain parts of the song, we could punch a lead in on the vocal track. I remember we wanted to get another solo on, so we stopped by Lloyd's house and hooked up some little fuckin' amp and just ripped through a solo. It was the first take. We went into the studio, and that solo ended up on the record. It's a fuckin' great solo, man!"

Although many stories claim Grant was actually a member of Metallica, James maintains that this single, slapdash encounter was the only time he was involved with the band. Other associates remember that Grant was a talented Delta blues player who had a knack for tasty leads. "He could play leads like a motherfucker," says James, "but his rhythm stuff was not very tight."

Despite Metallica's struggle to put this pilot effort together, "Hit

the Lights" had some major flaws, echoing their amateurism and inexperience. The song was efficient enough, with such innocently enthusiastic lyrics as "No life 'til leather, we're gonna kick some ass tonight!," but "Hit the Lights" was crippled by grimy production and Hetfield's croaky vocals, the result of the frontman's bout with a throat infection.

The song, however, was anchored by an amazing guitar sound: riffing so fast and grating that it threatened to peel the skin. Hetfield's guitars didn't just fill space, they chopped, stabbed, and cut like an elaborately-timed orchestra of firing guns and buzzing saws. During the final stretch of "Hit the Lights," a monster riff lurks beneath Grant's closing lead. With both its strengths and its weaknesses, the song was earmarked for placement on Slagel's pending compilation. Metallica would soon see vinyl.

✠

The cover, with its coating of Crayola crayon silver and cloud of floating skulls, looked like something one might find gathering dust in the corner of a cheesy occult bookstore. *Metal Massacre* hit the shelves on June 14, 1982. Ordinarily, the event would've been a major coup, but much had happened, rendering the compilation's release a trivial footnote.

First and foremost, Metallica's personnel had gelled. Hetfield doubled as rhythm guitarist and vocalist (but preferred, for a while at least, to act only as a singer in live situations), Mustaine served

Above: First Metallica group photo, 1982. L to R - Hetfield, McGovney, Ulrich, and Mustaine. Opposite: Flyer from Long Beach concert at The Bruin Den, August 7, 1982.

as guitarist, Lars remained as dummer, and McGovney was coaxed into playing bass. Musically, they churned out three more songs: Mustaine's "The Mechanix," with muscular, choppy riffs and lyrics that appear to tell the story of a horny gas-station attendant; "Motorbreath," a song Mustaine later called "Metallica's national anthem," with galloping riffs and "live-fast-and-die-hard" lyrics; and "Jump in the Fire," with lively, snake-like guitar parts and a Ramones-style bridge that showed the band's talent for arranging multiple riffs within the context of a single song.

As they'd done earlier with "Hit the Lights," the band accented these songs with Hetfield's relentless riffing. The distinguished musical brew that Metallica were refining as "their sound" was partly inspired by their influences. While their predecessors in metal such as Led Zeppelin and Black Sabbath had copped the moves of black bluesmen and subversive jazz musicians, Metallica had the New Wave Of British Heavy Metal to fall back on. Diamond Head and Motorhead had been Metallica faves since the beginning, but even more aggresive units like Tank, Venom, and Mercyful Fate galloped through the floodgates in an equally impressive fashion. Hetfield reflects back on the importance of such groups: "A lot of that stuff was way ahead of its time. The amazing thing about the NWOBHM was that England's not the biggest place in the world, so all these bands were from the same place, yet they had their own sounds. Today, there are a lot of Bay Area bands that sound the same, and a lot of Seattle bands that sound the same, but back then, everyone had their own style, which was great."

Hetfield cites Motorhead and Venom as two particularly influential cornerstones. "Those were the two bands that really helped us get aggressive. Their style was attack-oriented. Venom were way ahead of their time. They were too fuckin' heavy. They were more of an attitude than a band, actually. But they sure fuckin' rocked. They made a lot of fuckin' noise for three guys!"

Metallica had brought this unique brew of sounds to a handful of L.A. clubs, beginning with their first performance at Radio City in Anaheim on March 14, 1982, but the crowds had trouble dealing with this subversive new strain of music, which conflicted with the uptempo "happy riffs" of fashionable glamsters like Ratt and Motley Crue. Adding to this no-win situation was the simple fact that the band was showing their green. Mustaine, for example, broke a guitar string halfway through "Hit the Lights," after which the embarrased band retreated backstage to restring the instrument before starting the opening song all over again.

"There was no experience there," recalls Hetfield. "We didn't know what to do. Tell a joke [while the string was being fixed]? What the fuck did we do? We learned a lot at that gig, though. I don't think anybody from the band had gotten up on the stage before and played. Maybe Dave, in his previous band, but I know Lars hadn't. I had played at a couple of parties, but I don't think Ron had played before, either. Everyone was pretty fuckin' new, very green on that stage (laughter)."

On their "Denim and Leather" tour, UK cult metal heroes Saxon ravaged L.A. on March 28, at the Whisky-A-Go-Go; Metallica opened for the band, playing two shows that same night. In addition to their four original compositions, the brash foursome let loose on a collection of NWOBHM songs, including such Diamond Head numbers as "Am I Evil," "The Prince," and "Helpless." Still, the crowd receptions were lukewarm, at best.

To beef up their lineup, they recruited Brad Parker to play second guitar for their fourth show at The Concert Factory in Costa Mesa on April 23. "It was really funny," says James, recalling their only appearance as a five-piece band. "The rhythm guitarist hadn't played in a while, and was freaking out when the club announcer called us on stage. He goes running onto the stage, rarin' to go, and we're up there tying our shoes and shit, still tuning our guitars." Parker, who used the pseudonym "Damian Phillips" onstage, left the band after that sole live encounter and eventually joined Odin, another L.A.-area band.

Mustaine at L.A. gig opening for Saxon, March 28, 1982.

Although Metallica was back to its original four-piece format, its members still liked the idea of a second guitarist. To make this possible, James assumed rhythm guitar in addition to his vocalist's duties, a dual-assignment that he continues to this day. His first rhythm-guitar-and-vocals live performance was delivered on May 25, at Lars's school, Backbay High, in Costa Mesa. They played on a theatre stage, on which a kitchen backdrop had been erected. "It was a house setup, with different rooms," explains James with a laugh. "Some of us would get changed in the kitchen, and one of us might tune guitars in the living room. It was pretty funny."

Three nights after the shows at the Pantry, in a bottom-of-the-bill performance at The Concert Factory, Metallica found themselves in the unflattering position of opening for Los Angeles also-rans Leatherwolf, August Redmoon, and Roxy Roller. With crowds unreceptive to their crunchy live attack, Metallica defiantly speeded up the pace and turned up the volume.

By the time *Metal Massacre* was released the following month, the band was indifferent. "Hit the Lights," featured last on the disc, sounded like shit, and a typesetter had misspelled the band's name on the sleeve as "Mettallica" (also misspelling Ron's last name as "McGouney," an error that had the other members teasing the bassist for months). Although the band recorded a "new-and-improved" version of the song for future pressings, in which Mustaine played guitar leads, the debut was disappointing.

Despite their indifference at the time, however, the band would later count their *Metal Massacre* experience as pivotal to their career. "They say that if they'd never had the opportunity to be on that album, they might not have been a band," comments Slagel. "At the time, they were completely against everything that was going on in L.A. They would have had nowhere to play. All of a sudden, *Metal Massacre* gave them an incentive to appear on record and be a 'real band,' so to speak." The album went on to sell 30,000 copies. Ten years later, Metallica would chalk up over 10 million records sold. Things would change.

✠

One day in July 1982, Slagel was ready to close up after a day of work at Oz Records when John Kornarens rushed in with a tape. "See if you can guess who this is?" asked Kornarens, slapping the tape into a cassette player and turning up the volume. A surge of hammering guitars filled the store—a huge, chugging noise that pulsated with stubborn finesse. Slagel couldn't place the band, but he knew there was something special about this mad scientist's brew of steamroller guitar sounds, featuring forceful, distinctive

Opposite: James on stage during "...And Justice For All" tour, 1989.

gnashing of rhythm guitar strings. Metal music had taken a new form here. "It's Metallica," revealed Kornarens with a grin. Slagel's jaw dropped. "You're kidding," he blurted. "They're really good."

An early band flyer from The Concert Factory.

Metallica's *Demo Era*, was the outgrowth of the band's conclusion that since trendy L.A. crowds didn't appreciate them, it was time to distribute their music beyond Southern California. In June, they recorded a demo consisting of four songs and began distributing it to the underground network of metal fans. In the meantime, Lars plugged the band in metal fanzines, sensing that good, old-fashioned grass-roots promotion might be Metallica's only chance of gaining a larger following.

Patrick Scott vividly recalls teaming up with Lars to write the first-ever Metallica fanzine article, a one-page L.A. Heavy Metal blurb that would appear in Quintana's *Metal Mania* later that summer. Sprawled out on the floor of Lars's bedroom, the fledgling rock journalists conjured up their most "metallic" adjectives and exaggerated praises. "Metallica have the potential to become U.S. Metal Gods!" screamed Scott in that first write-up. He remembers the two laughing wildly over this unlikely prophecy.

With the demo's distribution network and a few articles in the metal press, Metallica was on a bit of a roll. But Lars, dissatisfied by the small-scale publicity, immediately coordinated the recording of a larger, improved demo tape called *No Life 'til Leather*. Financing for the tape came from Kenny Kane, the owner of an independent punk-label called High Velocity who had heard a live tape of the band playing some of their shorter cover songs. Thinking the songs were originals and liking what he heard, the entrepreneur reserved studio time for recordings to be released on his label as an EP. Soon after the recording session began, however, Kane was mortified to hear the band playing longer, more metal-oriented songs like "Metal Militia." Asking why they weren't playing the earlier material he'd heard on tape, the band responded that what he'd heard were cover songs. A furious Kane, who thought he'd be getting punk material and not the fast metal being churned out, ranted out his discontent, but he was stuck: the studio time had already been paid for. "We kinda fucked him up there," says Hetfield, "but he kinda had to do it."

No Life 'til Leather rehashed the band's four older songs and added three new ones: "Metal Militia," another "Metal is the Message" track that boasted Metallica's fastest riff ever; "Seek and Destroy," a slower song stealing from Diamond Head's "Dead Reckoning;" and, "Phantom Lord," which featured "repent-or-die" lyrics like "Fall to your knees...and bow to the phantom lord!" Glued together by the hammering riff effect that had already become Metallica's trademark, *No Life 'til Leather* topped the wish lists of global tape-traders. Scott laughingly remembers seeing Lars store the demo master tape on the top shelf of his bedroom closet after learning that, for proper storage, it should be "kept away from dust, metal, or anything magnetic."

The demand for the addictive Metallica became intense nearly everywhere outside of Los Angeles. *Aardschok* magazine, from Holland, gave the band a rave write-up. A tape trader from the unlikely frontiers of Oregon even called Lars to praise the tape and ask permission to start a Metallica fan club. Scott, acting as distribution coordinator for Lars, kept busy supplying the increasing waves of requests for tapes.

All this activity, however, didn't alleviate the band's primary snag—they were still trapped in the glam-obssessed realm of Southern California. Motley Crue were riding high on the success of their debut album, *Too Fast for Love*. According to a popular story, Lars walked up to the group one night at the Troubador and defiantly screamed, "You guys suck!," leading towering bassist Nikki Sixx to throw the pint-sized critic across the room.

The reality of this story, however, was much less dramatic, as James recalls: "I was there, and that's not exactly what happened. We were outside a club, sitting on a parked car, pissed off and drunk. We didn't even have enough money to get into the show, so we were sittin' outside, trying to weasel our way in somehow, meet someone, you know. Then those guys [Motley Crue] come walkin' out with high heels and grandma's jewelry on. They walked by, and we yelled, 'You guys suck!' They turned around like tough guys, and just stood there. They looked like fuckin' giants, 'cause they've got their Elton John heels on. Meanwhile, we're standin' there in our fuckin' tennis shoes goin' 'huh?' (laughter). They flicked a cigarette on us and walked away."

The excitement of Metallica's success on the underground tape circuit was further neutralized by the humbling reality of the band members' day jobs. Lars held a paper route for a while, then had a stint as a gas station attendant. But even these minimum wage endeavors were solely undertaken to accommodate his music.

"Lars had this gas station job," confirms James with a grin, "where he worked in one of those little booths where you'd go to pay. Dave and I would hide underneath there, blasting music and drinking beers when Lars was supposed to be working. On his paper route, he had to go out at four or five in the morning, so I'd help him pack papers and throw 'em. During the route, we'd carry a little recorder around and yell riffs into it [which would be used for songwriting later]."

Meanwhile, Hetfield made his spending money first as a high school janitor and then as a stock cutter at a sticker factory. "It was basically like cutting paper," he explains of the latter job, "only sticky. You'd cut it down to size for the customer, with this huge blade that would come down. One day, this codder pin had come out of the safety lever, and the blade fell on its own. Luckily,

Opening for Saxon at L.A.'s Whisky, March 28, 1982 (note James without rhythm guitar).

my arms weren't in it. After that, I said, 'Fuck you guys, I ain't workin' here anymore. I think I'd like my arms (laughter)!' Then again," he theorizes, "a one-armed singer might have been the next big thing in L.A.!"

Live gigs became easier to get, but they still felt out of their element and unappreciated. At the Bruin Den on August 7, they opened for Roxx Regime, later to become Stryper, the much-loathed practitioners of "Christian Metal." Nicknamed "The Yellow and Black Attack," the headliners decked out their mic stands, risers and backdrop with stripes of their repellent colors, in a theatrical stage display that Metallica tiptoed around during their opening set, looking disgusted and out-of-place.

The event's one saving grace was a bit of humor supplied by Hetfield when he borrowed the other band's microphone. "We didn't have our own mics at that gig," James recalls. "I basically used whatever the club had, but this wasn't a club. It was some kind of a hall, where you bring all your own P.A. We used [Roxx Regime's] mics and P.A. and gave them some money for it. I remember using their singer's mic during the show–it was some hot, special cordless mic I'd never seen before. The guy told me when I was done singing to turn the thing off. After the show, we were all drunk and sweaty and just left the stage. I left the mic sittin' there and forgot to flick the switch off! So the battery ran out—he went up to sing at his gig and he had no mic (laughter)!"

Another gig defining the group's anxiety and boredom of the local scene was played at the Troubadour on August 2. After charging through a surprisingly well-received set, the band were asked back out for an encore. Having exhausted their limited supply of originals and standard cover tunes, they huddled backstage, panicking over what to play. Lars's first choice was the frantic Diamond Head cover "Helpless," but the rest of the band, who barely knew the number, demanded "Blitzkrieg."

With the encore decided, they went back onstage and were surprised to hear Lars tapping out the beats of "Helpless." Metallica struggled through the barely-rehearsed piece. Backstage, an enraged James thanked Lars for his inconsiderate stunt with a punch in the stomach.

"That was one of the few times I threw my weight around," assures James ashamedly. "I didn't like to do that too often, but we were both real aggresive and full of vodka. It was the kinda thing where you were friends, so it was okay to hit each other."

✠

Brian Slagel came to the rescue from L.A. with the announcement that a place on the bill was available to Metallica for a *Metal Massacre* promotional show he'd organized in San Francisco. The prospect of getting out of Los Angeles had the band speeding off in a Ryder truck toward greener pastures up north on September 18. Eager to consume audiences at The Stone in San Francisco with their furious sound, they were unaware of the astounding surprises that lay ahead.

NORTHERN EXPOSURES

METALLICA'S FIRST gig in San Francisco, at The Stone on September 18, 1982, saw them sandwiched between headliners Bitch and show-openers Hans Naughty. An audience of over 300 had assembled, and it was immediately clear that the crowd wasn't there for the generic Naughty boys. "When Hans Naughty was on stage," recalls Marrs, now official Metallica drum tech, "everybody sat with their backs turned to the band."

This changed when Metallica bounded on stage and ripped into "Hit the Lights." As they peered into the frenzied blur of sweaty bodies and bobbing heads, the band realized this was their night. Armed with Metallica's demo tapes, crazed fans had mastered the band's entire catalogue of songs and were singing along. L.A. had never been like this.

"It was our first encounter with real fans," acknowledged James. "It was like, these people are here for us, and they like us, and they hate the other bands—and we like that 'cause we hate 'em too. These people appreciated us for our music, and not because of how we looked, which was how L.A. was."

By the time Bitch appeared with their S&M-style theatrics, the club had emptied, with most patrons heading outside to talk with Metallica.

✠

When Metallica weren't practicing, they'd most likely

Opposite: Dave Mustaine, The Stone,
San Franciso, March 5, 1983

be indulging in their second favorite pastime, drinking. In fact, drinking was an intrinsic part of their existence–while the band wouldn't be dubbed "Alcoholica" until years later, they were worthy takers of the title from their inception. "We used to get plastered and play," remarks James unapologetically. "That was our life! We hated people, and life, and everything. So we'd go into the liquor closet, find some booze, and we'd play as fast as we could and as loud as we could. Everything was okay after that. We felt great."

The passive Los Angeles vibe the band were trapped in caused volatile emotions. Fights occasionally erupted. The worst of these occurred between Hetfield and the unpredictable Mustaine after the latter's two pit bull pups leapt onto McGovney's Pontiac during a band get-together. According to Marrs, Hetfield gently brushed the dogs off the vehicle with a flippant remark such as, "Get off the car, you stupid dogs." The proud pet-owner, however, ran out and punched him in the mouth. McGovney emerged, jumped on Dave's back, and the scrap was soon broken up.

"Dave was actually kicked out of the band for about a week," recalled Marrs. "James, at least back then, never forgets. I don't think he ever forgot that incident." As the months passed, Mustaine's moods would cost him his job.

✠

Metallica stormed San Francisco a second time, playing the Old Waldorf on October 18, 1982, at a "Metal Monday" showcase. Even more bangers showed up to worship their new-found idols, and openers Overdrive met with the same fate that had befallen Hans Naughty. This gig marked the debut of "No Remorse," which, with its heavy grafting of plentiful lead breaks and progressively faster riffs, prompted more ecstatic headbanging.

✠

Ten days later, back in L.A., Brian Slagel encountered a phenomenal bassist named Cliff Burton. Trauma, an able metal fivesome from San Francisco, headlined the Troubador on October 28. Band promo posters boasted a "16,000-Watt Sound System and 60,000-Watt Lighting System," and "The Loudest, Brightest, Heaviest Show Ever!" Trauma almost lived up to the hype with their well-choreographed, dual-guitar team waving their instruments in synch. Apart from the bombast, however, stood the hairy, swivel-necked head of the denim-garbed bass player.

"Cliff had this amazing personality, banging his head throughout the entire gig," remembers Slagel, who arranged for Trauma to appear on his second *Metal Massacre* compilation. Slagel's admiration for Burton would prove crucial to Metallica.

✠

Yet another *Metal Massacre* night was scheduled for Thanksgiving at the Troubador. Like the last event, the showcase was for those featured on the album. The evening's schedule had Metallica sandwiched between Pandemonium and the Judas Priest imitators Malice. Recalls Slagel: "That was the first show where I thought they had *really* gotten good. They totally blitzed the place."

It was also at this show that Slagel realized that Los Angeles simply would not respond to Metallica's aggressive sound and presence, both of which were labeled "punk-like." "I remember talking to a promoter afterwards who said, 'They're a punk band. We don't have time for punk bands.' I thought, have you lost your mind? No one in L.A. understood what was going on."

✠

Later that month, a melancholy Lars phoned Slagel to outline his discontent with Ron McGovney. While he, James, and Dave formed an effective writing trio, McGovney seemed detached. To fire him, however, would cause discomfort since he and James were roommates. All the same, Lars felt something was missing.

Slagel, with visions of Burton's mop-top mane still dancing in his head, suggested Lars check out Trauma, who were scheduled to hit the Whisky-A-Go-Go. Lars took his advice, and in the smoky confines of the Whisky saw Burton appear on stage like a typhoon of energy, his wispy hair darting about like an Oriental kite flown by a particularly spastic owner. Lars and James, mesmerized by Burton's odd on-stage personality, sat awestruck.

"I could just see them go, 'Oh, my God! Look at that guy!,'" recalls Marrs, who was also there. "The thing that struck them most was that while you see lead guitar-playing, here you had a guy playing lead bass! They thought that was great."

The two admirers wooed Cliff after the show, but their initial attempts to lure him were in vain. In Lars's mind, however, Cliff would join the band. It was just a question of when.

✠

The Waldorf, with its personal, laid-back atmosphere, was a favorite hang-out. Thus, on November 29, Metallica found themselves headlining the Waldorf for the first time. The audience response was so frenzied that the band immortalized the night on a live demo tape entitled *Live Metal up Your Ass*. A new song, "Whiplash," was introduced by a drunken Mustaine with a touching monologue that recalled the first time he'd ever headbanged. The night was also memorable because the ferocious Exodus didn't get the "backs-of-audiences" treatment. Their guitarist, Kirk Hammett, would soon play a major part in Metallica's evolution.

The next evening, Metallica played a benefit on behalf of *Metal Mania*. Sloppy, improvisational playing and a loose vibe marked this fourth Bay Area show. "They ended up doing all kinds of weird shit that night," recalls Marrs, "like they weren't even caring." Obviously, the band was feeling increasingly comfortable with the city that would soon become its home.

✠

At this point, Lars's primary goal in life was to win Cliff over, a goal he pursued via a non-stop barrage of phone calls and in-person pleas. Burton finally gave in, saying he'd join the band under the condition that they relocate to San Francisco. But the process took time.

"Lars had to do a lot of wheeling and dealing to wear Cliff down," recalls Slagel. "Originally, Cliff didn't want to join because he had his own thing going with Trauma. It wasn't like Metallica just went up and told him, 'Hey, be in our band,' and he said, 'Oh, sure.' It took a couple of months to even get him to jam with them."

The magic surrounding that first jam session, which took place on December 28, 1982, was vibrant. The band camped out at the home of Mark Whittaker, Exodus's manager. Equipment was set up in primitive fashion in a small front room. With amps plugged in, instruments strapped on, and Lars perched intently behind his trapset, the band jammed for several hours. Cliff, his fingers flying over the frets, left his new comrades breathless. The chemistry was solid enough for Cliff to officially join Metallica.

A few days later, back in L.A., Hetfield, in a phone conversation with a friend, mentioned the band's plans to install Cliff. The conversation was overheard by McGovney's girlfriend, Colleen, who quickly passed the news on to a very pissed-off, newly ex-bassist. McGovney then approached James with the news that he was quitting. "There are two stories regarding how Ron left the band," says Marrs. "You talk to James, he was kicked out. You talk to Ron, he quit."

In an interview with Ron Quintana three months later, the band reflected on the bassist exchange in greater detail. "Ron didn't contribute anything," claimed James. "He just followed."

"A bass player is supposed to follow the drummer," continued Mustaine, "and Ron would follow the guitars. Ron could never follow what we did, and would copy us. Then we came up here and played with Cliff, who just blew the doors off of anyone we've ever played with. He's the new Steve Harris [Iron Maiden's much-

Lars in San Francisco, 1982

heralded bassist] of metal."

The band was particularly taken by the innovative newcomer's solo style, a lengthy mix of psychedelia, metal, and classical experimentation reminiscent of guitar soloing. "His solos are fantastic. They've got Bach and Beethoven in them, as well as rock, metal, and some Pink Floyd-type shit. Cliff's bad-ass."

Hetfield went on to second the notion. "The first time we jammed with Cliff, I wanted to ram through the fuckin' wall. He blew my mind. He fits this band like a glove."

✠

Cliff Burton, tall, mustachioed and sporting a Misfits' "grinning skull" tattoo on his right shoulder, had always projected the vibe that he absolutely didn't care what anyone else thought of him. Burton, who wore flannel shirts almost exclusively and was rarely seen without a cigarette in one hand and a beer in the other, began playing the bass guitar in 1976. In a *Metal Mania* interview by Harold Oimoen, he looked back on his pre-Metallica days.

"I used to jam around with some friends, then I got together with these guys who called themselves 'EZ Street,' named after a strip joint in San Mateo. They played all kinds of weird shit. We did a lot of covers, just wimpy shit. But I was with them for a while, for a few years. Slowly but surely, that disintegrated. Then I saw Trauma and thought, well, I might as well do that. Didn't have anything better to do."

By 1982, Cliff had played with Trauma on a two-song demo tape. One of the tracks, a bouncy, high-energy ditty with surprisingly catchy harmonies called "Such a Shame," appeared later that year on Slagel's second *Metal Massacre* compilation. By the time Lars began pushing him to defect to Metallica, Cliff had already grown restless with the more theatrical, commercial tendencies of his band.

"Eventually, Trauma started to annoy me, so I said, 'later.' It was musical. It was starting to get a little commercial, just different musical attitudes that I found very annoying."

When asked if he was frustrated by his own desire to get heavier, Burton replied plainly, "Definitely." When he joined Metallica, he got his wish.

✠

On February 11, Metallica became a Bay Area band, moving in with Mark Whittaker. The band eventually convinced Whittaker to defect and become their road manager, sometime-producer, and all-around coordinator. While Cliff continued to live with his parents, Hetfield, Mustaine, Ulrich, Whittaker, and official house dog Clive bounced merrily off the walls of the El Cerrito establishment, which quickly became the center for a thousand parties.

✠

Metallica's following grew at breakneck speed. Among the hardcore devotees were some whose fanaticism was particularly notable; one guy was even commended by the band for doing bodily damage to himself at gigs. It is alleged that, during one show, he headbanged so hard that he was hospitalized for whiplash. At another gig, he sustained a black eye after smashing into the back of another fan. Metallica eventually immortalized him by quoting his impassioned phrase, "Bang the head that doesn't bang," on the back of their first album.

"I remember this guy lit my couch on fire a couple of times," says James, conjuring up nostalgic memories. "He'd fall asleep with a cigarette in his mouth. I'd have another buddy sleeping on the other couch. We'd be drunk, but I'd be worrying about both of them. One would end up almost choking on his own barf—I caught him choking once, and had to turn him over—while the other would be threatening to light the fuckin' house on fire after falling asleep with a ciggie. We escaped death many times."

The record industry buzz on Metallica remained strangely muted. Despite their confirmed standing as the number one club band in the Bay Area, only a few independent labels jumped in with proposals; Metallica, however, refused to sign. Then Johnny Zazula, an enormous, bear-like entrepreneur from the East Coast, entered the picture.

Zazula, or "Johnny Z," was another of heavy metal's "outside-the-system" heroes. He was an East Coast Brian Slagel. In l981, Zazula and his wife Marsha worked out of a booth at an indoor market in East Brunswick, New Jersey, selling box sets of Jimi Hendrix, Cream, the Doors, and other late-'60s reliables. But then the husband-wife team got wind of the New Wave Of British Heavy Metal, and soon were hooked on its stable of ultra-noisy artists. Sensing that these new bands, with their leather, blue jeans, and scraggly, cosmetic-free appearances, might well be the closest thing to vintage '60s rock the new decade would have to offer–the Zazulas dedicated their booth to obscure metal. They published

Cliff at The Stone, March 5, 1983 - First show ever with Metallica.

James at the Keystone Palo Alto 1983 "Kill 'em All For One" tour. Opposite: Set list first S.F. show, September 18, 1982.

top ten lists of their most popular records in underground publications, trumpeting the work of such relatively unknown acts as Angel Witch, Anvil, Venom, and Accept. Zazula's collection of raucous records, coupled with his eccentric image as the untamed, Grizzly Adams of rock 'n roll, made him a huge celebrity.

Metallica legend has it that a customer slipped him a cassette copy of *No Life 'til Leather*. Without expecting much, Zazula slipped the tape into his deck. When "Hit the Lights" came blasting out, the big man's eyes widened to Ralph Kramden-esque proportions and he ran from his store in a Metallicized state of traumatic shock. He headed straight to a phone booth and called the band to heap praise on their heavy heads.

However embellished the above story may be, Zazula did contact Lars and convinced him to have the band travel east, where he vowed to assist them in finding shows and recording an album.

On April 1, 1983, Metallica jumped into a U-Haul truck and drove across the country to meet their latest supporter.

✠

On and off the stage, Metallica represented four very different types of characters. Mustaine was the talker; his stream-of-consciousness banter could by turns be incisive, intelligent, authoritative, or insulting. Live, it was Dave who supplied most of the between-song raps, and best understood the arrogance it took to convey a lasting image. Once in an uncharacteristic moment that is almost touching, Mustaine summed up his love for, and total devotion to, Metallica: "To be in this band, you have to be committed. I'd live and die for our music."

Creating the "proper image" probably ranked last among Cliff Burton's concerns. While the bassist looked Satanically possessed on stage–thanks to his convincing hair-curling routine—he appeared studious, understated, and poised before and after gigs. Fans who admired his generosity and friendliness, regarded him as an earthy musical blood brother. But he could also be unpredictable and crude. Burton concluded a fan club equipment rundown sheet he'd written with an obscene poem, followed by the philosophical post-script: "Control your life through insanity."

Hetfield was another chameleon. Interviewers happily indulged his marked fondness for good jokes and good vodka. But he was also fond of exercising firm control. The dominating lyrical and musical force in the band, James was quiet around others. But when he did speak, his words spoke volumes.

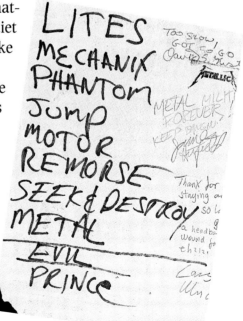

Lars, musical and mental athlete, and originator of the band, remained its driving force. As one who devoted all his energy to Metallica, he was ill-disposed to the idleness in the others. The physical runt, Ulrich was Metallica's unlikely mover-and-shaker, the band watchdog who would pull his mates to their feet when they seemed out for the count.

The entire group knew how to have a good time, but they all also sensed the importance of control. All that is except one.

✠

On April 11, 1983, Dave Mustaine was, as Lars said soon afterwards, "given the elbow." In an interview in *Metal Mania*, Lars summarized the events that culminated in Mustaine's departure and Kirk Hammett's appearance as their new guitarist.

"James and I have always been the main thing in this band, and we always looked at Dave and Ron and thought, 'This is fine for now, but...' We had a vision that these guys weren't gonna last. We weren't gonna kick them out, but if we happened to find someone who could fit in, we'd get 'em in the band. We saw Cliff and went, 'Whoa! This guy should be in the band!' So we concentrated on him until we got him.

"It was the same situation with Dave. One night in the beginning of March, me and James were talking. In the background was a tape of Exodus playing, 'cause Mark [Whittaker] was their manager at the time. We thought, 'Wait a minute! It almost sounds like there's a real guitarist there! Sounds pretty good, like what we're looking for in terms of fast metal!' I'd seen 'em a couple of times, but when you're seeing them and you're thrashing about it's different than when you sit down and listen to them on tape. That was the first time we'd thought about it. Then the next couple weeks it was like, 'Kirk! Kirk! Kirk!' It wasn't as if we were gonna put him in the band and get rid of Dave...until we left for the East Coast later that month.

"We were driving along in the U-Haul 'limo,' having a wonderful time sleeping in the back and shit, when we ran into some problems—around Iowa and Illinois—involving a drug called Alcohol & Dave. Dave got really drunk. He'd probably had 15 or 20 beers and was driving the truck while we were crashed out in the back. He almost killed us 10 or 15 times! About seven o'clock that night we stopped to eat, and Dave and Mark got into a heavy fight. Everyone was sober except Dave, and after a while, he passed out in the back. The four of us were in the front, talking about how this guy isn't stable enough to be happening on the road. He's a great guy and a great friend, but he just couldn't handle his alcohol. So that night, just out of Chicago, we shook hands and decided this was the end, and that we'd get Kirk."

On April 11, the band was camped out in New York at a ramshackle rehearsal pad, a couple of days after playing two gigs with Vanderburg and The Rods, when the final blow was dealt. The band members cringed at the thought of confronting Dave with the unpleasant news, but the announcement was inevitable. Lars, who couldn't afford a plane ticket for Dave, had bought a Greyhound bus ticket for him instead. The bus was scheduled to depart at 10 a.m., making it necessary for the band to dismiss the troubled, chemical-gobbling muso early at dawn. The rest of the Metallicrew huddled up at 8:00 a.m. sharp and set their change-of-guitarist strategy into motion.

"Everybody was bummed out," explains Lars, "but we'd decided James was gonna tell him. It was such a weird scene, as everyone was looking up at the ceiling or down on the floor like somebody died, or was about to be executed. James tapped him on the shoulder, woke him up, and said, 'We've decided you're not in the band anymore.' Dave looked around the room; he must have thought he was dreaming. He said, 'Oh, no!' After 10 or 15 minutes of our telling him why, he realized he wasn't gonna get us to change our minds, and he made the statement of the year: 'Okay. When does my plane leave?' He had three days on the bus to think about it. He was sad, but I think the way we did it was really good, because we only spent an hour or so from the time we told him until we actually waved good-bye.

"James and I were in a real low mood afterwards, 'cause we'd spent a year and a half with the guy, spending every day together. So we got some bottles and got drunk and went sightseeing [in New York]. Then Kirk arrived. He'd had our tape for a week or two to practice with, so we went in about two a.m. that night and started jamming. The guy played about five notes and it sounded so completely different! Me and James looked at each other and smiled—that initial feeling was so good and so different. We'd never played with anyone who knew what he was doing, which

Dave and James indulging in their favorite offstage pastime, S.F., 1982.

was great because we'd gotten him out there without even knowing if it would work out...we took a chance. We jammed for a couple of hours—it was great! We got the set down by Friday and played a couple of gigs that weekend, then a couple more with Venom the next week, a gig in Baltimore, then one with Prey and later Anthrax."

In a subsequent interview with Trace Rayfield in *Whiplash* magazine, the band explained their Dave-dumping in greater detail. Mustaine's tendency to drive while under the influence was

First-ever photo session with band lineup of Burton, Ulrich, Hetfield, and Mustaine.

but one of many reasons for his departure. James made this abundantly clear as he compared the sacked guitarist with his successor: "Kirk's got Dave's speed, but Dave was all speed. He had no feeling, he had no pull-offs, he had no brilliant things. He tried to get brilliant sometimes, but it would sound awful."

"It was more like Dave was playing for girls, and to tell his friends he was in a band," added Lars. "I'll tell ya, this guy Kirk, he wakes up in the morning and he just plays—I mean all the time. Dave would only play when he wanted to. It wasn't like he played guitar 'cause he wanted to. It was more an excuse to show off."

While Metallica clearly came to bury Mustaine, there was also some praise: "Dave's real fast and talented, though," said James. "I doubt if he's gonna quit playing."

✠

Indeed, Dave didn't stop playing. In a matter of weeks, the unapologetic Mustaine had rebounded with Megadeth, in which the domineering sorcerer blasted forth his trademark runaround rhythm patterns and heavy chords while singing and stirring a 'deth cauldron of spiteful lyrics and skillfully-constructed compositions. In songs like "Love You to Deth" and "Skull Beneath the Skin," you could almost hear him demanding vindication from anyone who might be foolish enough to cross his vengeful path. But even as he replicated the magic Metallica climb from relative obscurity to major-label record prominence, Mustaine had to battle a host of professional and personal obstacles.

But he prevailed, riding his genius for riff-writing, dry wit, and a verbal facility unheard of in headbanging. By the summer of 1992, Megadeth's fifth album, *Countdown to Extinction,* debuted at number two on the U.S. album charts. He also emerged as a successful father, capable of juggling on-the-road jet-setting with the more intimate, domestic routine of a family man. During a July 1992, interview conducted by Brian Lew exclusively for this book, Mustaine confided the joy he felt upon hearing his two-year-old child call him "daddy." Eight years after Metallica, his life happily in balance, Mustaine reminisced about his former band.

Can you reflect on the first gig Metallica ever played?
I remember I spit beer into the P.A. columns and speakers. I was squirting beer from my mouth onto the speakers 'cause the promoter was such a dick.
Any memories of the first Metallica rehearsal?
Before the rehearsal, I went to Lars's house and he played me the tape of "Hit the Lights." I said, "This song sucks! You need more guitar solos." And Lars went, "Oh, fuck, mon—reeeeeaaaalllly?!" (laughs). I convinced him that I should be in the band and went to rehearsal. I was tuning up when all the other guys went into another room. They weren't talking to me, so I went in and said, "What the fuck? Am I in the band or not?" And they said, "You've got the gig." I couldn't believe how easy it had been and suggested we get some beer to celebrate. Then we started learning cover songs...Diamond Head, Sweet Savage, and Blitzkrieg. But at that time, I can tell you pretty much what we were drinking, and that's about it."

What was the story with Brad Parker [Metallica's second guitarist during their only gig as a five-piece]*?*

He used to call himself Damian Phillips on stage, and wore spandex and mascara, and played a Charvel Star Body guitar. He thought he was Randy Rhoads. He had a great-sounding amp—when he wasn't there. He looked more like Joanie Cunningham ["Happy Days"] with red hair. We didn't think he was the right guy for the band, but James didn't want to play guitar. I'm really happy that he started playing guitar.

What are some of your impressions of the first Bay Area gigs?

The thing that blew my mind was the great times we'd have riding back from the concerts. We'd have a half-gallon of cheap vodka that we'd pour into each other's mouths, totally hammered 'cause we'd gotten in [to San Francisco] and gotten out alive. We were disgusted with Ron McGovney at the time, too, and so we decided that on every road trip home we would throw one of his shoes out the back of the truck. We would always get back to L.A. and he'd only have one shoe!

Describe Ron McGovney's split with the band.

He knew that we were planning to fire him, so he quit. Lars and James may deny that, and Ron may say he totally planned it, but we had planned on firing him.

It was really weird, what took place at that time. I was starving and selling drugs to keep myself alive. There was never any food at rehearsal [at Ron's home]. James was starving. He'd given up some job as an artist. I think he was doing advertising or something. So we would always raid Ron's refrigerator, and the fucker always left, like, one tomato and a half a loaf of bread in there. But the cruelest thing was when we'd steal his liquor and fill the bottles back up with water. By the end of the night Ron was drinking five proof vodka and we were drunk as skunks. There were so many times there that I'd wake up in this chair by a pool table with lipstick all over my face, 'cause they'd written "666" on my face after I'd passed out. It was one of those things where you take advantage—the empowering of the unempowered—as soon as one guy goes down, you kick him a couple of times.

What's your impression of Metallica now? Are you happy with the way things turned out?

I miss them a lot. It comes and goes, and sometimes it's painful and sometimes it's very vindicating. I know there are two great bands now, but it makes me wonder if I was still in the band how much farther they would or would not have gone. Inasmuch as Kirk is a great guitar player, I think there was such a difference in

Cliff in Europe with a copy of Metal Mania.

our playing [that the styles would've complemented one another]. I know James is an excellent rhythm guitar player, but two heads are better than one. I think, though, aside from us [Megadeth], that Metallica are probably the best band at what they do. In the Eighties, we wrote a certain chapter—thrash/speed metal—but in the Nineties, it's the New Age of Heavy Metal. It's come full circle. It says in the Bible that a dog returns to its own vomit. Well, we're back to basic barf!"

✠

Kirk Hammett, raven-haired and fair-skinned, dove into a raw phase of hiding out in a shady Queens rehearsal studio, eating poorly, and living a "subterranean lifestyle" while his new band

recorded their debut platter. Such an existence was a far, far cry from the one back home in Berkeley, where he'd wielded axes for Exodus on such furious power-metal hymns as "Impaler," "Die by His Hand," and "Hellsbreath," and spent his remaining time flipping patties at Burger King to raise money to buy guitars.

Lars and Dave Mustaine reunion in S.F., 1988.

Before joining Metallica, Hammett's musical experience wasn't extensive. After forming Exodus in 1981, with drummer Tom Hunting and recruiting guitarist Gary Holt, bassist Jeff Andrews, and singer Paul Baloff, Hammett played on a demo tape recorded a year later that featured the speed metal anthems "Death And Domination," "Whipping Queen," and "Warlords." As Exodus performed regular club shows, the guitarist gained a reputation as the six-string kingpin of the Bay Area.

Kirk's longtime friend John Marshall, who in later years would become the former's on-the-road guitar technician, remembers being at a party where Kirk summoned him to break some special news. "He told me, 'You're not gonna fuckin' believe this,' recalls Marshall, "'but I'm supposed to go out and join Metallica tomorrow on the East Coast!' He was leery, though. He thought that Mark Whittaker might have been playing a prank on him."

Hammett, who broke into the band during an April 16 gig at New York's Showplace opening for The Rods, soon realized that

the invitation was no joke.

✠

Owners of the *No Life 'til Leather* tape were already familiar with the basic tracks on *Kill 'em All*, but they were pleasantly surprised by some lyrical improvements and altered song arrangements. The "auto-erotic" silliness of "The Mechanics" was nixed when the song was lengthened and re-titled "The Four Horsemen." The evil narrator of "Jump in the Fire" speaks "From the depths of my fiery home," instead of blathering gibberish about needing to "get up, get off, get down." Burton tore things up in a studio incarnation of his bass solo entitled "Anesthesia/Pulling Teeth." James, with his sandpaper rhythm guitar, dominated the grooves throughout the record, inventing a new metal style and setting the standard for future chord-thrashers. Within two weeks, *Kill 'em All* had sold over 17,000 copies, an unheard-of figure for an independent release. It would be 10 years, however, before the disc would show up in such "respectable" places as

Rolling Stone's "Top Records of the Eighties" edition, go platinum, and rightly be hailed as an all-time masterpiece of trend-setting rock music.

Making the record had its low points, however...many of them. When recording started, the group had taken residence with the Zazula family, but they were banned from the house after raiding the liquor cabinet and downing the couple's cherished wedding champagne. "They'd been saving it forever," recalls an unrepentant James. "We popped the top and drank it. That was it." After this

Original lineup of McGovney, Hetfield, Ulrich, and Mustaine in S.F., 1982.

unacceptable offense, Metallica spent the next few weeks slumming around at a horrid dive in the middle of Queens called The Music Building. "It used to be a furniture warehouse," reveals James. "It was eight stories of rooms that had been turned into a rehearsal place, and it was in this fuckin' really bad, drug-infested neighborhood. We had to live there! We had no transportation, we had no fuckin' money, no food—it was pretty bad. The guys in Anthrax helped us out with a refrigerator and a toaster; they were practicing there, too. There was nothing but fucking cold water in the sink."

As if these circumstances weren't dire enough, the band were locked out of the mixing room while Zazula and his co-producers twiddled knobs at *Kill 'em All*'s birthplace, Music America Studios. As a result of such repressed conditions, the band was disappointed in the final product. James recalls that Burton was particularly miffed. "Cliff had all kinds of shit that he wanted to record on his bass, and the producers would say, 'Well, it doesn't sound

right.' Of course it didn't sound right! It wasn't fuckin' normal! But it's how we wanted to sound. Those guys were too fuckin' sterile. We were out there trying to create new sounds, and they were shootin' us down from the beginning."

The release of *Kill 'em All* in the summer of 1983, was followed by another masterful coup–the breakthrough "Kill 'em All For One" tour, which saw Zazula's two biggest acts, Metallica and Raven, take to the road together for the first full-fledged indie-label tour. Beginning in New Brunswick on July 27, and finishing off, appropriately, on the band's 'Friscan home turf, the historic "tour de (Mega)force" gave Metallica national exposure. But, it wasn't an easy haul.

Once again risking life and limb in a customized Winnebago that gave out before the tour had finished, the band survived both the attacks of rabid, urban Metallicrowds, and the less character-istic confrontations with shotgun-wielding Oklahoma mountain men out to "teach them longhairs a little respect."

A particularly rural stop saw the band playing Bald Nob, Arkansas. "Bald Nob was a cement slab in the middle of nowhere," describes James. "There were more bugs than people. They set up catfish stands, and that was about it. Our music was a little too rough for them, no doubt, but it was a good time."

With an album and a tour tucked under their stud-encrusted belts, Metallica were home to party. But the pleasure was dis-tracted by business, as they wrote new material and continued, rung by excruciating rung, up the ladder of heavy metal infamy.

Above: Kirk Hammet with pre-Metallica band Exodus. Opposite: (top) James in S.F., November 1982. (bottom) Metallica with Raven, September 1983 at end of "Kill 'em All For One" tour.

THE ROUGH ROAD TO ELEKTRA

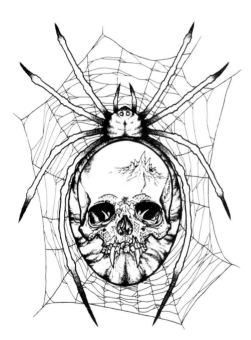

THE END OF the "Kill 'em All For One" tour marked the beginning of John Marshall's career with the band. A hulking, six-foot, seven-inch friend of Kirk Hammett's, Marshall initially came aboard to help out with tasks as simple as keeping the guitars tuned. The casual, soft-spoken, dark-haired Goliath ended up playing babysitter, tour manager, replacement guitarist, guitar technician, and victim of abusive English road crew members.

Metallica abandoned San Francisco in November of 1983. After headlining three shows opened by Armored Saint, held on November 25, 26, and 27, in Palo Alto, Berkeley, and San Francisco, respectively, the band hit Los Angeles, Chicago, and New Jersey. They were killing time, building their domestic following before going on a European tour with Venom.

Life on the road, at the time, was primitive. Marshall remembers the group being so low on cash that they had no flight cases for the amps and instruments. The band's minimal equipment consisted of four Marshall cabinets and two bass heads, with the guitars plugged directly into the amp.

So impoverished were they that Marshall remembers eating an average of one meal a day. Without money for decent hotels, the band and crew would take refuge with

Opposite: Fine dining with Metallica, 1984; this was also the first photo session by longtime Metallica lensmen Ross Halfin.

fans like Metal Joe, who had converted his Old Bridge, New Jersey house into a "charity hall for the bands."

After the Left Bank gig, John remembers sacking out with Kirk Hammett at Joe's pad and unsuccessfully trying to get some sleep. Exhausted, the slumbering guitarist and equipment tech were jarred awake by music blaring through the floorboards from the basement below, where Joe was running his stereo through a huge P.A. system. A roaring New Year's party was in session, but with Joe and others supplying the roof over their heads, the Metallica entourage only had hunger to sort out. Marshall remembers fans buying them meals, and on Christmas Eve, a female admirer took them to a fancy restaurant, paid for the sizeable meal, and left. On the way out, the group was accosted by their waitress, furious because she hadn't tipped her. "She freaked out, yelling and all pissed off," recalls Marshall. "But we would barely have eaten that day if it hadn't been for that meal."

A blizzard that mirrored the harshness of Metallica's current tour blanketed Boston as the band's road crew pulled into the city on January 14, anticipating a gig at the Channel Club that night. But the severe snow storms caused the show to be cancelled. With the band stuck in New Jersey, the disappointed road crew parked alongside a hotel and checked in for the night. The falling temperatures, however, were worrying John. Fearing that the extreme cold would warp the guitar necks, he unloaded the guitars and stashed them in his hotel room.

The next morning, John was alarmed to look out his window and see that the Ryder truck was gone. Broke and hungry, the crew was faced with the news that their equipment truck, and contents, had been stolen. Mark Whittaker notified the Boston police, thinking that they might have towed the truck for being parked illegally, but such was not the case. Among the hot-wired vehicle's contents were Hetfield's prized amps, integral to his *Kill 'em All* rhythm sound, Lars's Camco drum kit, and numerous amp cabinets and pieces of stage equipment. The guitars that Marshall had salvaged, including James's white Flying V and Cliff's red Rickenbacker bass, were all that remained.

"Someone must have seen the guitars being unloaded the previous night," said Marshall, reflecting back on the theft. "The next day, someone drove in from New Jersey to pick us up. We were all sitting in this sedan, with guitars under our legs, taking this five hour drive back to New Jersey, and everyone was miserable 'cause the gear was gone."

To this day, Hetfield remains puzzled by the theft. "If it was

James unplugged, at the
El Cerrito Metallipad, 1984.

such a blizzard, who the fuck would be out there? Hardcore criminals? Maybe the cops just took it away. Who knows? Maybe our gear's sittin' in some police station somewhere."

For the remaining three gigs before the band's anticipated trek overseas, Anthrax loaned Metallica their stage equipment. The group's anger over the theft only fueled their performances through New York and New Jersey before they stormed back to the scene of the crime, Boston's Channel Club, to make up the gig that had been cancelled. "If any of you know the fuckers who stole our equipment the last time we were here," announced James from the stage, "please kill them for us." Meanwhile, Megaforce Records issued a global alert notifying the metal-going public of the theft, but no sign of the truck or the equipment would ever be reported.

✠

The "Seven Dates of Hell" tour, on which Metallica supported Venom, gave Europe its first taste of the band as they blasted through Switzerland, Italy, Germany, France, Holland, and Belgium playing with rented equipment. The tour almost came to a halt as soon as Metallica arrived at the first gig, however, where Hetfield fell down holding a beer glass and cut his hand open.

On February 11, in Zwolle, Holland, they played to 7,000 militant, hardcore headbangers at the Aardschok Festival. Aardschok—the Dutch word for "earthquake"—was legendary for its association with *Aardschok* magazine, an influential fanzine. Although Venom, with their extravagant crosses-and-pentagrams blend of Satanic doom-rock closed the show, Metallica, with their

unpretentious, no-frills stance, made the greatest impression with the frothing audience.

Lars backstage at The Stone, 1984.

For the last show of the tour, both bands played in a stripped-down cafeteria in Belgium, on a stage made up of hinged-together tables. As an obnoxious going-away present for their openers, Venom loaded Lars's trapset with talcum powder, causing an explosive cloud to form whenever the unprepared drummer hit a snare drum. In addition, the bratty Newcastle headliners unhinged Cliff's section of the stage, which left the bassist off-balance, causing him to struggle through the set.

✠

On February 20, the day the band's new found European label Music For Nations issued the *Jump in the Fire* EP (including hilarious "live" versions of "Seek and Destroy" and "Phantom Lord," which allegedly had been recorded at the Bay Area's Automat). To cash in on their momentum, Metallica entered Sweet Silence studios in Copenhagen, Denmark, to begin work on their second album, *Ride the Lightning*. Before recording began, however, the band endured the painstaking task of finding James an amplifier that could match the electric, in-studio crunch of its stolen predecessor.

"They literally looked at every Marshall amp in Western Europe," recalls John. "They eventually found one that sounded good in some little Danish music shop."

The album's first four songs had been written the previous winter, shortly after the "Kill 'em All For One" tour was wrapped up. A demo including this new material was thrust down the reliable underground pipeline and instantly gobbled up by fans. However, the tape's reception was accompanied by quizzical head-scratching. While an opening track called "Fight Fire with Fire" unloaded itself like a lethal firecracker and proved their fastest song ever, songs like "Ride the Lightning" and "When Hell Freezes Over" (later known as "Call of Ktulu") were slower, lacking the breakneck pace of the *Kill 'em All* blinders. With extended middle sections, fleshed-out harmonies and accoustic intros, the new material certainly showed that Metallica was growing–but would the progression be welcomed by their fans, who had been raised on speed, speed, and more speed? Another song on the tape, the forceful "Creeping Death" (which lifted its "Die by My Hand" chorus from one of Kirk's old Exodus songs), was a solid metal epic, but even it lacked the grating, cheese-shredder crunch.

The band had begun their first ballad, "Fade to Black," in January while hanging out on the East Coast before the Venom tour. The bad luck suffered by Metallica added depth to the downbeat song. But news that the one-time speed kings might be mellowing out, first with the unusual demo material and then with a gentle ballad, made fans nervous. Their reaction made the band jittery, if not a bit angry.

After being told that the demo tape sounded surprisingly different from their previous recording, Ulrich sighed. "I hate hearing that. I can't help but worry about what other people think [of the new material], but I shouldn't worry, because I feel like we're playing for ourselves, and if we wanna do a ballad, or whatever, we'll do a ballad. If people don't like it, fuck 'em.

"I think the musical change has happened quite by itself. It wasn't planned. Most of the *Kill 'em All* songs were written in the spring of 1982, and we really didn't have a clue what we were doing musically. We've learned so much since then. We have two people in the band that know a lot more about songwriting and harmonies and shit like that than the two previous people. Now it's four people writing songs instead of just two.

"This ballad we're writing is pretty different. There will probably be a few hardcores who will go, 'What the fuck?' and be totally against it, just 'cause they don't understand that you grow and mature. They'll want us to just keep playing open E chords for the next three years. But I think we'll gain a wider array of fans with this material."

The band was pressured to exit the studio with LP master tapes in hand by March 14, giving them less than a month to record. This situation was particularly stressful considering they still hadn't finished writing the material for the record; as a result, tracks such as "Trapped Under Ice," "For Whom the Bell Tolls," and the unusually commercial "Escape," were written on the spot between recording sessions.

The resulting album was a dark, muscular-sounding cornerstone for the band. "Fight Fire with Fire's" understated acoustic intro opens up to a turbulent rhythm-guitar hammering and Hetfield's vocals, which cry out the consequences of nuclear war in a chant reminiscent of Discharge's relentless punk masterpiece, "Hear Nothing, See Nothing, Say Nothing." "Ride the Lightning," the mid-paced title track, explores the final thoughts of a law-breaker sentenced to die in the electric chair, with claustrophobia-inducing lyrics like "Flash before my eyes/Now it's time to die/Burning in my brain/I can feel the flame." "For Whom the Bell Tolls," the album's pinnacle, builds from a creeping-spider riff into a swaggering soldier's march. The song's layered architecture would provide the structural blueprint for most of Metallica's dynamically charged future songs.

"Fade to Black," the infamous ballad, was the last-words confessional of a suicide victim. The song would eventually go on to strike up controversy with right-wing types who deemed it "pro-suicide," a description the band would vehemently reject. Its personal lyrics, which also secured the band the following of female fans who'd had trouble dealing with the bang-your-head sentiments of *Kill 'em All*, touched a universal nerve. It was difficult to fathom anyone not relating to the track's final, surrendering verses:

Things not what they used to be;
Missing one inside of me.
Deathly loss this can't be real;
Cannot stand this hell I feel.
Emptiness is filling me;
To the point of agony.
Growing darkness taking dawn;
I was me but now he's gone.

"Fade to Black" was the band's most daring cut in another respect; its slow, acoustic format, only occasionally interrupted by anything resembling a heavy riff, saw the band abandoning their speed-metal roots in favor of subtlety and depth.

That summer, *Ride the Lightning* was released on Megaforce Records in America and on Music For Nations in Europe. It garnered positive reviews and was received by an amazed headbanging clientele that applauded Metallica's move into a realm of far-reaching dynamics and varying styles of music. It spawned a 12-inch single, "Creeping Death," for which the band recorded a potent B-side duo of cover songs, Diamond Head's "Am I Evil," and Blitzkrieg's "Blitzkrieg."

James on stage in Europe.

✠

By the time *Ride the Lightning* was down the pipeline, Metallica had dropped Megaforce Records, sacked Johnny Z., and signed with Elektra Records; they hired Q-Prime management at this time as well. The band has always been vague regarding the exact reason for the transition, but one can assume that Megaforce's increasing stable of other bands, like Raven, Anthrax and Exciter, simply resulted in less time for Metallica matters. Meanwhile, the band found the financial security available at a major label to be particularly desirable.

The turning point came during an August show in Roseland, New Jersey, where both Elektra and Q-Prime approached the band simultaneously. "A couple of Elektra's A&R guys [including Michael Alago, who would ultimately sign the band] were at that show," remembered Lars in an interview with Brian Lew for *Crucible* magazine, "and they were down in our dressing room after the gig. The next thing we knew, we were having dinner with them, and a couple of days later they were dealing with us." Meanwhile, the Q-Prime duo of Cliff Burnstein and Peter Mensch, perhaps the most respected and efficient hard rock team in the industry, took the band under its able wings. By August 12, Metallica had officially signed with Elektra Records and Q-Prime, shedding their indie-label skin.

✠

It was around this time that the Spastik Children phenomenon began. During the rare slivers of free time that Hetfield was granted at home between touring and recording, boredom and an urge to play in a setting removed from his Metallica persona prompted him to join a party-band called Spastik Children. Com-

prised of Fred Cotton on vocals, James McDaniels (aka "Flunky") on guitar, and a bassist named Jumbo, the unit of lovable drunks invited James to play drums, an offer which he accepted with much delight.

The concept behind Spastik Children was simply to have fun in as un-professional a context as possible: songs were written on-the-spot during practices, musicians preferred playing instruments they had no past experience with, and the band hosted a revolving-door policy of members that would come and go as they desired. Cliff Burton joined, and Kirk Hammett had his turn. According to James, if the band had any kind of a mission, it was merely to "get as drunk as possible and see if we could still play, and abuse the crowd. That was the whole object."

Meanwhile, if the audience made the sorry mistake of re-questing Metallica material, they were spit on, sworn at, and

Above: Kirk on stage in Europe 1984. Opposite: Lars wearing silver spray paint at the El Cerrito Metallipad, 1984.

generally degraded. "People would come and ask for 'Creeping Death,'" explains James, "and we'd say, 'Fuck you, dick!' They wanted to hear Metallica songs, which is not what we were there to do."

On the tour front, some changes were made in the Metallica camp. Q-Prime restructured the Metallica road crew, adding new roadies and excusing others. Robert Allen, for instance, a Q-Prime mainstay who'd helmed tours for the management company's most recent success story, Def Leppard (Allen is also the brother of Leppard drummer Rick Allen), was assigned the road manager's post, and several of his English cronies filled the other crew spots. As a result, John Marshall was forced to brave the band's 1984 European "Ride the Lightning" tour which started in September, as the lone Yank in the crew.

The tour made 26 stops, and before the final show at the London Lyceum on December 20, Marshall observed some genuine strangeness. Fans, paying homage to "Call of Ktulu," tossed H.P. Lovecraft books inscribed with sinister symbols on stage. Meanwhile, Marshall spent a considerable amount of time being terrorized by his English crew-mates, who made the American the butt of their cruel pranks.

"English humour is very harsh and sarcastic," notes Marshall. "Being the only American, I got tons of shit. I was kind of miserable, now that I look back on it. I even got pissed on in my bunk by a drunk lighting guy. I woke up thinking I was sweating, but it turned out to be piss. He was really ripped, and I think the other English guys had whispered to him, 'Hey, man, go down to that American's bunk and piss on him.'"

Hetfield later confirmed that the offending bladder belonged to Tony Zed, and claims that Kirk was also doused in his bunk that same night! "Kirk will deny it to this day," reports James, "but I saw it. I think the guy got both Kirk and John. He had a lot of fuckin' beer in his gut!"

Marshall was also dubbed "Condor" by the relentless Brits. The nickname, he explains, refers to an English ad campaign for Condor tobacco pipes, in which a man is shown gazing dreamily through a window. The accompanying catch phrase reads, "It's a Condor moment."

"During a ferry ride they'd caught me staring out the window in a daze or something, just like the pipe ads, so from then on they called me 'Condor.'"

At the end of the tour, Robert Allen presented the humiliated guitar tech with a commemorative pipe. "It took me two fuckin' years to realize he was pulling my leg by buying that pipe," laughs John good-humoredly. "Even now, years later, I'll go, 'They were fuckin' pulling a joke on me!'"

✠

With the advent of a new year, the group was summoned back on the road to promote *Ride the Lightning*, with a series of gigs co-headlined by WASP and Armored Saint. The convoy began on January 10, 1985, at the Channel Club, where visions of stolen equipment no doubt flared up in Metallica's memory banks. To add insult to recollected injury, Lars was sent back to Copenhagen after forgetting his work visa, and the band had to sit the gig out. Amazingly, the jet-lagged drummer made it back for the following gig in Scotia, New York, the very next evening.

While the Metallica/Armored Saint camaraderie grew stronger on the road, the band's relationship with WASP was a strange, lopsided affair. WASP frontman Blackie Lawless treated the other bands with a reclusive indifference born initially of arrogance and later embarrassment. Things fell apart for Blackie as soon as the tour hit its third stop in Hartford, Connecticut.

"Some kid in the audience had a sign that said, 'Blackie Ball-less sucks!,'" recalls Armored Saint singer John Bush. "Blackie spotted it and was getting pissed, so he spit on the guy. Then the guy conjured up this loogie from hell, and it nailed Blackie right in the face! Metallica and us were on the side of the stage roaring, and he looked over and gave us this look of doom."

"From then on," adds Saint bassist Joey Vera, "Blackie never spoke to us." From the East Coast, the tour headed to Canada, and Metallica had acted as tour headliners to this point, playing last every night. Upon hitting the frozen north, however, WASP protested that they sold more records in Canada, and should be granted the headlining slot. Metallica obliged, putting WASP in the terrifying position of following their fireball performances.

"They got killed every single night," recalls Bush. Back in America, both bands compromised on headlining status by swapping positions every other night, through Buffalo, Cleveland, Chicago, Detroit, St. Louis, Kansas City, Iowa, New Mexico, and Denver. At a sweaty Phoenix show, a promising young bassist named Jason Newsted marvelled at Metallica; it would not be his last glimpse of the band.

During their few days off, the bands conducted bouts of "raging," in which vodka flowed freely, hotels were terrorized, and pranks were pulled fast and furiously. Armored Saint vocalist Joey Vera later described the "Jacket-elevator-fire-extinguisher" incident that made him and James infamous to hotel managers across the country:

"We were raging one night in Denver when James came into my room, wanting to try on my leather jacket. As he tried it on, he walked towards the window saying, 'This is a nice jacket. Let's see

"Alcoholica" in classic form.

how it flies!' He tossed it out the window, and it landed by the pool. We went down to retrieve it, and when we were coming back up the hotel elevator, we decided to pull out its emergency stop button. This set off an alarm. We tried pushing the button back in, but nothing happened. So the elevator was stuck, literally, between two floors, security was screaming at us to get out of the elevator, alarms were going off and James was going nuts.

"Then we crawled out of the elevator onto the hallway of the floor below. James picked up a fire extinguisher from off the wall and aimed it at me. He started fuckin' squirting it, there was fog all over, and the sensors picked up that someone had shot off an extinguisher, so the fire alarms started goin' off all over.

"I snuck back to my room, and out the window, police cars and fire trucks were pulling into the hotel parking lot, and people were being evacuated outside in their pajamas and underwear. A lot of people got pissed off, 'cause there was a convention in town, and half the clientele packed up their bags and left and the hotel lost all kinds of money. James ended up having to pay a fine."

As could be expected, the tour's final stop at Portland, Oregon's Starry Night Club on March 19, brought the raunch and rowdiness to a peak level. John Bush found himself handcuffed to the stage by Metallica in mid-set. In a fair exchange, Bush and his Saint cohorts jumped onstage during Metallica's "Metal up Your Ass" chant and dropped their drawers. The audiences enjoyed a fine view of a row of pale butt-cheeks, before both bands jammed on a punky cover version of Fang's "The Money Will Roll Right In."

Cliff on stage in Europe.

FROM MASTERS...
TO MOURNERS

THE ARRIVAL OF the summer of 1985 gave the band the opportunity to rest up and begin throwing around concepts for their next album. The relaxation came to an abrupt halt, however, when they embarked on a series of festival appearances. First up was the Castle Donington "Monsters of Rock" festival in the UK, where Metallica would play to 50,000 English fans.

Since Donington was considered a "one-off," and a complete tour crew hadn't been assembled, John Marshall assumed responsibility for shipping gear and equipment to London and chauffeuring the band around Great Britain. He drove the band, learning to drive on the opposite side of the road, to Birmingham on August 13, to rehearse for the Donington show.

"All the guys were in the back getting pissed drunk," he told an interviewer, recalling the band's excited response to arriving in England. "Cliff was in the front, crankin' the stereo and poundin' on the fuckin' dashboard. I'd stop to look at a map, and they'd all stagger out to take a leak, after which I'd have to round them all up and kick 'em in the ass to get back on the bus."

The Donington show was held on August 17, and Metallica was fourth on a bill that included ZZ Top, Marillion, Bon Jovi, Ratt, and Magnum. Fans crowed over the fact that Metallica was billed above Ratt, the innocuous

Opposite: "Master of Puppets" tour
photo session, 1986.

platinum-sellers from the image-conscious streets of L.A. Aware of the strong contrast that existed between the bands, Hetfield remarked midway into Metallica's set, "If you came here to see spandex, eye makeup, and the words 'Ooh, baby' in every fuckin' song, this ain't the fuckin' band!"

James takes a break between tours on home turf in San Francisco, 1985.

Back on home turf, they prepared for Oakland's "Day on the Green" festival; slated for September 30, a crowd of over 60,000 was expected. A week before the show, however, the band paid homage to their "old guard" fans with an unannounced show at Ruthie's Inn, where they were billed as "The Four Horsemen." The intimate atmosphere was best evoked in a *Metal Mania* review.

Metallica Finally Make it to Ruthie's Inn!

On Saturday, August 24, a benefit for Ruthie's occurred with Terminal Shock, XX20, Ulysses Siren, and Control (who couldn't play because Doug Piercy was on tour with Exodus). The benefit was held to replace the $6,000 P.A. ripped off from the club.

Meanwhile, it was known that Metallica had wanted to do a warm-up gig before "Day on the Green," and rumors were flying. By midnight, all three bands on the bill had finished, and the Metallica guys started showing up. Barely 100 people were inside

Ruthie's, unsure of what was gonna happen until James, Lars, Kirk, and Cliff got onstage!

They came out to a frenzied roar and opened up with "Creeping Death," and a great knockaround time was had by all! James purposely made Kirk mess up, and vice versa, in between boogie jams. Cliff went full-roar, beating the fuck out of his bass. Lars was banging fiercer than ever. I've never seen him bang so hard; he was really intense!

Then the guys invited their friends to sing some old favorites. First was Fang's "The Money Will Roll Right In," starring Andy Anderson and others, followed by the classic "London Dungeons" by The Misfits, featuring Skitchy on vocals. Next was the standard "Blitzkrieg." A few were stage diving and skanking, but most were headbanging in front of the band.

"Dickrash" (a.k.a. "Whiplash"), "Motorbreath," and "Phantom Lord" continued the onslaught, pounding through with tremendous amounts of power. Metallica then turned into a frenzied "Alcoholica" and "Drank 'em All" at Ruthie's! "Drink and Destroy" (a.k.a. "Seek and Destroy") was next, as they played teasing riffs of Broken Bones, "Hot for Teacher," "Roadhouse Blues," "Smoke on the Water," weird, twangy country tunes, and other shit.

The epic "Am I Evil," and magnificent "Fight Fire with Fire," finished off the 90-minute set in grand thrashing style, as nearly everyone sang along.

Lars shaving his tongue at the El Cerrito Metallimansion in 1985.

✠

Metallica's "Day on the Green" performance a week later was a "hometown-boys-make-good" celebration, and an antidote to the overbaked posturing of other bands on the bill—like Yngwie Malmsteen, Ratt, Y&T, and Scorpions. Y&T, who at one time ignited the Bay Area music scene with such impassioned, all-American hard rock albums as *Struck Down* and *Earthshaker*, were now adorned in silk suits and accompanied on stage by a bulky, plastic robot mascot. Meanwhile, Metallica mopped around in torn jeans and dreadlocks, talking to fans and downing beers–in observable contrast to the "limo-and-sunglasses" crowd–before waking up the sun-baked California kids with a solid set. Highlighting their performance was Cliff's throbbing bass solo and a tight rendition of "For Whom the Bell Tolls" (both of which appear on the video compilation *Cliff 'em All*).

This first "Day on the Green" appearance also marked the first of Hetfield's many harsh encounters with legendary Bay Area promoter Bill Graham, when the psyched frontman gleefully trashed Metallica's backstage trailer. "Me and some of my rowdier friends were so fucked up that we were throwing fruit around. We'd throw the fruit, and they'd explode on this grating, a vent that would go into the next trailer, so the juice would spray all over whoever happened to be in there. So we were throwing all these things, and it got down to avocados, which were all that was left on the fruit tray. Somehow, the avocados wouldn't go through (laughter). So we took baseball bats and kinda smashed the vent apart. Then we went off on the furniture. The whole trailer got demolished, basically."

Graham was not amused. Hetfield was called into the intimidating icon's office and was scolded. "What happened in the trailer," reflects James, "was kind of what we used to do at our house [in El Cerito]. We'd throw parties and take all the furniture out of the place, so you could get wild without breaking stuff. If there was something there, it would get broken. So basically, we were treating the trailer like our home (laughter). But Bill didn't understand how we could treat things like that."

In an interview, Kirk expressed satisfaction with the "Day on the Green" gig, but said the band had trouble hearing themselves onstage. He spoke of spending his free time producing demos for such local metal bands as Blind Illusion and the speedcore, Death Angel. When asked about his current listening habits, Kirk cited Seahags, Sisters of Mercy, Warning, Loudness, Samhain, Metal Church, English Dogs, and Minor Threat as the bands most likely to be blaring on his Walkman.

The very next day following the "Day on the Green" show, Lars and James jumped on a plane and headed to Copenhagen, where they planned to lay down drum and guitar tracks for their forthcoming album, *Master of Puppets,* in the familiar confines of Sweet Silence studios. They were eventually joined by their Metallica comrades, who enjoyed a few more days resting at home.

✠

In late December, Metallica came home for the holidays. Opting to mix work with pleasure, they took on a gig opening for Y&T in Sacramento. On New Year's Eve, they headlined a powerhouse, hardcore metal marathon at the San Francisco Civic Center which also featured Exodus, Metal Church, and Megadeth. It was a bill made in thrash-metal heaven, but the event took an upsetting turn during the induction of the new year. "At the end of the gig, we were pretty fucked up, with the countdown, and all the balloons dropping and everything. We were singing some fuckin' thing, and we basically wanted people in the crowd to sing along, but I couldn't get the mic off the mic stand to throw it out. So, I took the whole mic stand and tossed it.

"The big metal base on the bottom kinda cracked some kid on the head. I guess he wasn't lookin' or something. He went to the first aid tent to get bandaged up, and then we took him backstage. We were really giving him the works: champagne, T-shirts, and that kinda stuff, hoping he wouldn't sue us (laughter)! A few weeks later, we got a call from some lawyer saying he was suing us anyway. We said, 'Fuck you—give us our shirts back. Ha, ha!'"

Upon hearing of the incident, promoter Graham once again

summoned the relentless troublemaker. "He got kinda rough with me," confesses James. "He couldn't understand how a band could be so violent. The whole aggression thing he was not into, because he was a real '60s hippie-type guy. He was pretty open-minded about things, but he just couldn't understand it.

"I remember he threw me out of his office, and he wasn't gonna book us any shows. Basically, I had to kinda come back in. He wanted me to come crawl to him. I thought, fuck it, he's the only guy that can book bands in the Bay Area. I came back in and told him, 'Hey, we're young and we're doing this because it's what we

Lars with Yngwie Malmsteen at 1985 "Day on the Green" festival in Oakland.

feel. And I don't think you can do anything wrong if you feel it. We're young and we're learning.' And he understood that, and said, 'Okay.'"

As quickly as they'd arrived in the States, the band then headed back to Sweet Silence to polish their new album.

Master of Puppets, Metallica's third album, was the product of five difficult months of studio effort. Stark, vivid imagery and a

Hanging out after hours with Exodus, 1985.

more compact production sound than *Ride the Lightning* made it a punchy, immediate record that tore the band's dynamic envelope open even further. There were the trademark fast songs, like "Battery" and "Damage, Inc.," which reprised the "metal is the message" attitude of older songs like "Whiplash" and "Metal Militia," only "three years later and three years better," as Lars proclaimed. There were also several "many-songs-for-the-price-of-one" musical marathons, like the title track–a wobbly train-ride into the hell of drug abuse. With songs like "Master...," Metallica achieved a lengthy, epic effect that replaced the stripped-down, three minute riff-a-ramas on *Kill 'em All*.

While *Master of Puppets* continued down the same progressive path taken by its predecessor, it seemed glued together by a cynical theme: the manipulation of the powerless by some sinister, all-knowing group. Its cast of unsavory characters—an evil melting pot of oily preachers, drug addicts, asylum inmates, mythical sea monsters, and order-barking generals—seemed the product of a distrustful, ultra-paranoid mind-set.

"We've been observing the way people get fucked around, sometimes without even realizing it," editorialized Lars during a fan club interview. "Obviously, there are many songs on this record that explore manipulation. 'Leper Messiah,' for instance, deals with people being manipulated into sending these people money, thinking they'll be able to meet God sooner, or meet God better. 'Welcome Home (Sanitarium)' was inspired by the *...Cuckoo's Nest* film—not directly, but somewhat. The whole thing is about hanging out at places like that and being told that you're crazy and insane, and that this is your home, where you belong, and feeling inside that these people are wrong."

In *Metal Mania*, Cliff Burton elaborated further on *Master of Puppets*. "'Master of Puppets,' the song, deals for the most part with the kind of things that happen when people get dependant upon drugs. 'Disposable Heroes' is more of a military-type thing, of what could and might happen to soldiers. Personally, I would say the 'Master' of this whole thing is Fate. Seeing the drug dealers alone as the masters is to look at it very narrowly, because they're just peddling their wares. I'm not really sure how James, who wrote it, looks at it. When I look at it, everyone gets ground under the wheels. Whoever is on the playing field is fair game, and it's up to them to avoid being used.

"'The Thing That Should Not Be' is another portion of the 'Call of Ktulu' mythos. It's about huge guys marching around! Huge fuckers so big that they compete with buildings in size! 'Leper Messiah' is our religious song; it's basically addressed to the television evangelist-type. Take your pick; they're all the same."

Master of Puppets was released on February 21, 1986. It immediately entered *Billboard*'s Top Thirty chart, and soon was certified gold. It was clear that a spot on a high-profile tour bill would be the one thing that could push the band even higher into the stratosphere. Enter Ozzy Osbourne.

Metallica's breakthrough to arena exposure came in the form of an opening slot for Ozzy Osbourne, during the ex-Black Sabbath

Flyer for Metallica's first "Day on the Green" appearance, summer 1985.

vocalist's "Ultimate Sin" tour. The image of James Hetfield holding club punters in his hypnotic gaze was suddenly magnified. When he chanted "SEEK AND...," the writhing masses responded with a deafening "DEEEEESTRRRROOOYYY!" It was clear that these concert-goers had known about Metallica for a while.

✠

Later in the tour, the vibe turned serious following a major injury. Marshall remembers relaxing behind an amphitheatre in Evansville, Indiana, where the band was scheduled to perform.

"I spotted Bobby Schneider [the band's tour manager at the time] and James, and James had this expression on his face like, 'Oh, fuck, this hurts!' Obviously, he'd hurt his arm, or something. Then Kirk ran up to me and said, 'Hey, man, you might be playing rhythm guitar for us tonight!' I kinda thought, gee, okay, not taking him seriously."

Marshall took the situation far more seriously when he learned that James had been hospitalized and sedated as the result of a skateboard injury. It was soon determined that the frontman's arm was badly broken. That evening, the other three Metalli-members announced to the crowd that they would be unable to play. They were met with chants of "Bull-shit! Bull-shit! Bull-shit!"

Before leaving for Nashville, where the following evening's show was scheduled, James stumbled back to the Mesker Theatre and gathered with his bandmates. With his plaster-covered arm requiring weeks of healing, Hetfield would be unable to play rhythm guitar. Q-Prime had cautioned the band that forfeiting the tour would mean losing a considerable amount of money. Beyond the cash factor, there was another issue: Metallica's integrity. The band panicked at the thought of another round of angry booing. But James described a scenario that would allow Metallica to continue the tour: he would simply sing, while a replacement rhythm guitarist would assume power-chord duties.

Among the names tossed around as a possible stand-in was Anthrax's Scott Ian. As fate had it, however, the honor would go to a different candidate; the ever-reliable, battle-scarred road dog extraordinaire, John Marshall. "The decision to have me do it," explains John, "was based, I think, on the fact that I knew all the parts. After all, I was the band's guitar tech. So when this other roadie and I drove the truck to Nashville, I played guitar to the *Master of Puppets* tape. I'm thinking, whoa, this is gonna be a trip; not that James had broken his arm, but that I'd get to play."

When the band arrived at Nashville's Hyatt Regency Hotel later that night, James coached the anxious "fifth member" through various tricks of the rhythm guitar trade, preparing John for his debut. When Metallica took the stage soon afterwards, John was hidden in a small compartment alongside the P.A. system, several feet behind the band.

"The first night I played about five songs," he recalls. "I think the band was afraid it wasn't gonna work. Lars told me later that he'd been real skeptical about it, and that it had taken him a few gigs to realize that it was gonna be okay. I couldn't play like James,

so it sounded different. As a roadie, you don't practice four or five hours a day; you tune up the guitar and play for five minutes.

"We'd open with 'Battery' and 'Master of Puppets.' James would run around the stage, just singing, with guitar parts mysteriously coming from nowhere. So after those first two songs, James would announce: 'Obviously, I'm not playing; we've got this guy down here who's playing guitar.' I'd walk out and wave, then go back to my little hidden corner."

John continued offering his rhythm guitar support for five more American gigs, at the end of which the band took a month off. As they had assumed that James's arm would heal in time for their

Back stage with Ozzy Osborne during 1986 "Master of Puppets" tour.

upcoming European headlining tour, the band panicked when their frontman's precious limb was still tender when September rolled around. Reasoning that what worked once would work a second time, they summoned Marshall. Beginning in Cardiff, Wales, on September 10, John and his towering frame once again shared the stage with Metallica, this time hidden behind one of the huge crosses that comprised the band's stage set.

"I was kind of off to one side where the crowd could kinda see me," he recalls. "As the night would go on, Cliff would look over at me and go, 'Get the fuck out here! Come out and play!' Four gigs into the tour, I was basically on the stage. I didn't move around too much 'cause I was really scared. I also felt kind of obligated not to do too much, since I was there to just play guitar."

John did 12 shows in Europe. Along with his playing duties, he continued his obligations as guitar tech. "I'd get there in the afternoon, help unload the truck, set up my amps, plug 'em in, do the soundcheck, put on stage clothes, eat dinner, do the gig, wave and walk off the stage, rest for a minute, start unplugging the amps, load them up, and haul them into the truck. I got paid double. I made more money in those three weeks than I ever made at one time in my life. Playing was fun, but it was hard, and I couldn't wait to get back to being a roadie."

By the time the band reached Stockholm, Sweden, on Septem-

James with photographer Harold O. showing off battle scars at S.F.'s Rock On Broadway club.

ber 26, the long hours of double-duty were affecting John's health. His diabetes, which required regular insulin injections, put a further damper on his well-being. Burned-out and battered, Marshall decided to resign when the tour ended in November.

James resumed his rhythm guitar playing that night. "They just slayed," recalls John. "It was the first gig in which James played guitar in three months, they were really up for it. They just fuckin' slaughtered."

The vibe that night was one of relief and recovery. The band was now one hundred percent a well-oiled machine. The next two months, in which the band was scheduled to conclude the tour and close the books on *Master of Puppets*, should have been a breeze.

James provides comic relief at a Bay Area party, 1986.

After the show, the band hopped on the tour bus and into their bunks for the long drive to Copenhagen. On board were the four band members, along with drum tech Flemming Larsen, guitar assistants John Marshall and Aidan Mullen, and road manager Bobby Schneider. The driver, an Englishman who had been hired for the duration of the multi-country tour, was seated at the wheel. About 6:30 a.m., the band members were awakened by a violent jolt. The vehicle was on its side. Bobby Schneider had shattered two ribs. Lars had broken a toe. Kirk's eye was blackened. Hammett, who'd blacked out after being thrown from his bunk, snapped to consciousness and made his way through a side emergency hatch. Outside, his eyes widened at the sight of Cliff, his body limp and lifeless, pinned under the bus. Cliff Burton, master bass player, composer, rager, and bandmate, was dead.

How did it happen? Marshall recapped the horror, and shed some light on the question of what, exactly, occurred.

"We were on a two-lane road," recalls John. "The bus went off to the right, and I think the driver overcorrected, cranking the wheel to the left to get us back on the road. The wheel grabbed, and the bus swung completely around to the point where it was facing back the way it came. During this time, the tail of the bus was sliding, kind of fishtailing around and bouncing on its wheels. That was right when we all started to wake up. I think I bounced right out of my bunk. The bunks were like trays with foam in them, with a little wooden lip around the foam that stood up about four inches. My back bounced across that lip, and by the end of the day, I could barely walk, it hurt so bad.

"The bus eventually slid to the dirt alongside the road, where the wheels caught, and it rolled over on its side. Cliff was on the top level of the right rear bunk, and I think that as the bus was bouncing around, he sort of pushed through the window; when the vehicle fell over on its right side, he was halfway out the window and it fell on him."

Meanwhile, the bunks toppled like matchsticks, teetering into one another and collapsing into a pile of kindling. Mullen and Larsen, who'd also slept in right side bunks, were pinned under the rubble for nearly three hours before the fire department jacked up the debris and rescued them.

"When the bus first stopped on its side," continues Marshall, "I remember hearing this noise that sounded like water. I was afraid we'd landed in a creek, and were halfway underwater. But the noise was only the motor still running."

Within minutes, Marshall and the band had pulled themselves from the bus and huddled outside. "We were all sitting out there in 35 degree weather, with me in my socks and underwear before someone gave me a blanket. I remember Kirk and James yelling at the driver. By then, everyone had begun to realize that something was wrong with Cliff. I remember James walking up the road a bit to see if there was ice on the road, after the driver had claimed he'd slid over a sheet of ice. Kirk was crying."

After being routed to the emergency room of a nearby hospital, John remembers coming to the realization that something was very, very wrong. "I remember Bobby Schneider lyin' next to me, as they were taking our blood pressure and stuff, and saying, 'Cliff's gone, you know.' All of a sudden, the reality of everything hit me. Right then, I looked above, at the ceiling, and thanked whoever was up there that nobody else had been seriously hurt, and that it hadn't turned out even worse than it was."

By afternoon, band and crew had checked into a hotel. The dazed group dealt with their anxiety in the manner they were most familiar with, drinking. James broke two hotel windows and screamed, venting his rage. John remembers that he and Kirk were so shaken up that they left the light on in their room that night. Two days later, Metallica, minus one, returned to America.

✠

An uncharacteristic silence seemed to veil the Metallica camp in the days that followed. Flowers poured into the band's fan club. The radio stations which had ignored Metallica's music now broadcast over-the-air condolences. The Bay Area papers were full of downbeat articles announcing the death. The music community—artists, rubber-treading road crew associates, record company executives, studio professionals and fans, all of whom felt a musical kinship with Cliff even though many had never met

Opposite: Cliff Burton photo collage, compiled by a long-time Bay Area friend Harold Oimoen.

CLIFF BURTON

him—mourned the loss of one of its own.

Cliff Burton, 1986

What was that eccentric, earthy charisma that made Cliff so unique? As someone who was brash and compassionate, twisted and studious—and scrupulously honest—Cliff cut a presence which few would forget. Shortly after the band completed their recording sessions for *Master of Puppets*, Harold Oimoen, a Bay Area friend of the bassist, conducted a casual interview with Cliff. Following are excerpts from that conversation:

Cliff, tell us what you thought of "The Day on the Green" show.

The crowd was fuckin' real good—real big. I was fuckin' real drunk. I guess we did okay. Fuckin' it's hard to tell when you're onstage, you know. You don't really know what's going on, you just do it and fuckin' find out what happens later.

What about the Donnington show and the bottles?

Donnington was a day of targets and projectiles. Fuckin' shit was piling high on the stage, and freaks were fuckin' flipping. They just do that because they like to.

What about the new album?

My favorite song is "Master of Puppets." I think it's the best Metallica song yet.

How did it go in the studio?

It took too long. The songs were real good, but we could have managed our time a bit better.

What do you have to say about the early days?

It was fun then, it's fun now. I think you could safely say we've matured musically, if not any other way, over the past three years.

What was your most memorable show? I imagine "Day on the Green" and New Year's Eve were especially cool shows because for massive crowds in your hometown.

You see, that's the thing. Different shows have different good points. It's really great to do a big show in front of the hometown, but there were other gigs where things were really, really happening. I couldn't pinpoint one as being my favorite.

How about naming your top five albums?

Well, let's just say top five bands. Everything by Glenn Danzig, which is The Misfits or Samhain. All of Thin Lizzy's stuff. The old Black Sabbath stuff. There's a band called R.E.M. that I like a lot and Aerosmith.

Who have been some of your influences?

My influences have been Geddy Lee [Rush], Geezer Butler [Black Sabbath], and [jazz bassist] Stanley Clarke. Lemmy [Kilmister of Motorhead] also had an influence because of the way he uses distortion.

Do you have anything to say to aspiring musicians?

When I started, I decided to devote my life to it and not get sidetracked by all the other bullshit that life has to offer.

Band at 3132 El Cerrito household, 1984.

METALLI-COMEBACK!

CHAPTER 5

IT WAS CLEAR that Cliff was irreplaceable, but the idea of breaking up Metallica seemed to go against the principles of the musicians who had proclaimed, "We'll never stop, we'll never quit, 'cause we're Metallica" ("Whiplash").

According to Brian Slagel, the three surviving members immediately knew who they wanted as a replacement. "A few weeks after Cliff died," explains Slagel, "Lars called me up and told me they needed a bass player. I told him I knew who the obvious first choice was: Joey Vera of Armored Saint. He was the first guy they called, but he didn't want to do it. I had numerous conversations with Joey, and he said that even though the offer was a great opportunity, he'd grown up with the Armored Saint guys, and they had a dream they wanted to fulfill. I told him that he had to go with what was in his heart. He passed, and I think Metallica understood why. So Lars asked me to keep my eyes open for other bassists, and to send any noteworthy tapes to San Francisco."

The auditions began in October. Metallica tempers were tested by every Bay Area wannabe within earshot of the well-publicized "bassist wanted" announcements. Some select candidates did emerge from the dreck, however, including Willy Lange of Laaz Rockit and Prong's Troy Gregory.

Opposite: James and Kirk, from the Garage Days Re-Revisited photo shoot, 1987.

But the gig eventually went to Jason Newsted, a Phoenix, Arizona, bassist and ringleader of Flotsam and Jetsam. Newsted was a one-man musical circus, acting as Flotsam's manager, primary songwriter, and all-around coordinator. His "jack-of-all-trades" versatility had won him a number of fans, among them Slagel, who had released two of the band's recordings and had found himself in a strange predicament: Newsted was on his label, and he valued the prized bassist's allegiance to Metal Blade. On the other hand, he believed Metallica should approach Jason, predicting a winning chemistry would develop.

"I called Lars and said, 'I hate to do this, 'cause they're a band on our label, but there's a guy in Flotsam and Jetsam who's really good.' I sent some of his tapes up. Then I called up Jason. The first thing I asked him was, 'Are you sitting down?' 'cause Metallica was his favorite band. Then I told him I'd recommended him to Lars for the Metallica gig. I think he was pretty much in shock."

The cycle of telephone calls continued when Lars called Newsted and put in a personal request that he audition. "I was pleasantly surprised," admitted Jason in a fan club newsletter, "and decided that I couldn't let the opportunity of a lifetime pass me by. I played many, many hours the next four days in preparation. The first audition was great–we seemed to really hit it off. I was asked to return for a second audition, and then asked to join Metallica.

The question was popped after Newsted was exposed to the

Jason Newsted (at far left) with pre-Metallica band Flotsam and Jetsam, 1985.

band's alter ego—the notorious "Alchoholica." Metallica hauled the unsuspecting Arizonian to Tommy's Joint, a popular downtown drinking hangout. Was Newsted compatible? Would he succumb to the dreaded Mustaine-itis after downing a few beers? As the night wore on, the three veteran Metallicans stumbled into the men's room, leaving Jason alone at their table. They reached a final verdict among the urinals. "I think he's cool," Lars slurred. "Do you guys think he's cool?" Heads nodded. Jason was in. Returning to Jason's table, Lars laid things on the line. "Do you want a job?" he asked the anxious recruit. Jason responded by yelling out a joyous scream that nearly scared off the restaurant's other patrons.

✠

Prior to taking on his allegiance to heavy metal music, however, Newsted lived a "domestic" lifestyle. He grew up in Niles, Michigan, in what he sums up as "a really good family atmosphere." He recalls life on a farm as being an all-American blend of sports, big relative get-togethers on the holidays, and raising horses. It was a secure existence, but his parents kept him busy, instilling a regimented work routine.

"My parents were very hard workers. They always set a real good example—you know, 'go-getedness.' My dad would always

Jason Newsted, 1987.

say, 'Take the incentive and don't sit around waiting for something to come around. You gotta get to it and take advantage.'"

Music was always a force to be reckoned with in the Newsted household. He remembers playing his older brothers' 45's of The Osmonds and The Jackson Five, and his father's prize investment and family-time centerpiece was a pedal-powered player piano. "That was the best, man!" he recalls, grinning. "My dad had a vat of these roles of player piano music. He was so proud of them. He'd buy a new one each couple of weeks. My dad would be sittin' there, rockin' to the song 'Alfie' [starts singing out loud, in an exaggerated barbershop-style croon 'What's it all about Alfieeeeeeee...']

"I'd like the songs that you played at faster tempos, like 'Saber Dance.' We'd get nutty on the songs we liked better. We'd speed 'em all the way up when mom and dad weren't home. Those were the ones that had the frayed edges (laughing). But the piano was something we always did. We'd sit around and listen to it."

When he was 14, Jason's family moved to Kalamazoo, where he attended a "different kinda high school, with a lot of real rich kids." Away from the rural lifestyle and close friends, the rebel instinct took over. "I started getting into trouble. I didn't like school anymore, and started listening to a lot of music, and buying records. I had a couple of jobs, making pizza and whatever, and I'd save up and just buy records." Then the bass bug hit Jason, who lived within five miles of the Gibson guitar company's original Michigan factory. "I ended up gettin' a little Gibson amp and a bass, because of Gene Simmons of Kiss. Myself and three other kids would pretend to be Kiss—I liked Gene the best."

When the 1980s new heavy metal wave steamrolled through the record bins of Kalamazoo, Jason caught on. "My brothers, who were so into Motown, had left for college, and I started finding other music. Heavier stuff like Motorhead, Thin Lizzy, and Tygers of Pan Tang. I can remember getting very serious about the bass: I'd have it sitting in its case every night, after I was done playing it, and I can remember dreaming about someday...[becoming a successful rock musician]. I guess that's an experience a million people have had."

Newsted saved enough money to buy a new bass and hooked up with a local band called Gangster, which played standard, party-metal classics by Ted Nugent, AC/DC, Ian Hunter, and Kiss. The group's guitarist, Tim Hamlin, became a mentor of sorts, teaching the aspiring rocker guitar scales and new bass techniques. In a move that shocked Jason's family, he quit high school three months before graduation. "Quitting school hurt my parents," he recalls. "I usually did good in school, until I went to this snooty school and stopped trying. My grades went down. But they still wanted me to go to college. I moved out of the house for a while, and in with the Gangster guys. I was real scattered at that time."

It wasn't long before Newsted headed for California, in pursuit of musical success. Traveling alongside Hamlin and his girlfriend, as well as a sheepdog named Rudy, Newsted strapped himself into a U-Haul truck and headed southwest. While the original road plan was full-speed-ahead to L.A., the road-weary clan took a pit stop in Phoenix. "We pulled in on a really nice, sunny day," recalls Newsted. "I can remember the hot winds of late, late October blowing." They never left.

Newsted broke himself into the new area by taking on a variety of odd jobs, such as working at a Subway sandwich store and washing dishes. "I drank a lot of coffee back then," he laughs. "But I could always eat 'cause I'd seem to always be working at restaurants. That saved me. I'd drive to work on a motocross bike."

He drifted away from Hamlin, and eventually got wind of drummer Kelly David-Smith after eyeing a classified ad the skinbeater had placed in a record store, which called for other musicians to jam with. "This guy wanted to play hard rock, and mentioned liking Van Halen and Rush. I took my stuff over there, and he was already jammin' with two other guys, guitarists. They already had a band name: Paradox. I jammed with them for a while, but they really never amounted to much."

As Paradox fizzled out, Jason and Kelly made a pact to form a serious band. "I was high, man–not from any drug, but because we were actually forming a real band. Kelly had this huge drumkit with cymbals and double-bass. We'd jam away in his dad's den."

Newsted eventually moved in with the ambitious drummer, in Scottsdale, and the pair recruited neighborhood guitarists Kevin Horton and Mark Vasquez. With Jason singing as well as playing bass, the unit dubbed itself DOGZ. Aside from Horton, who threw in the towel and was replaced by Ed Carlson, the lineup remained stable enough to play several parties and record a demo tape. "We did our first demo at an eight-track studio that Kelly's drum teacher had. We did a couple of cover songs, and a couple of songs Mark and I wrote, 'Dogs of War,' and 'Screams in the Night.' We thought we were pretty big shit."

DOGZ' only weak link was its vocal department. Newsted helmed the mic off and on, but a bona-fide singer had to be recruited. Enter Eric A.K., who joined the group in 1983 after impressing his bandmates-to-be with a vocal palette of wails and screams bringing to mind Judas Priest's Rob Halford. "When we auditioned Eric, he would come in and listen to Judas Priest tapes a couple of times, and then sing them–'WOAAAGH!'–way up. We're goin', 'No way!'"

DOGZ changed its name to Flotsam and Jetsam, after a term taken from the J.R.R. Tolkien book *The Hobbit*, and became local legends at such Phoenix-area clubs as The Mason Jar, Rascals, and Peoria. Then they cut into the familiar veins of the underground tape-trading circuit with a demo entitled *Metalshock*. The subtly-titled "I Live You Die," one of the demo's four songs, was pegged for a slot on Slagel's seventh *Metal Massacre* compilation in 1985. Soon afterwards, the band was signed to Metal Blade and churned out its debut album, *Doomsday for the Deceiver*. Like the band's previous material, *Doomsday*, combined the intricate, fast, stop-

James on stage in Japan, 1986.

start riffing of bands like Metallica and Slayer with the comic-book imagery of Iron Maiden and Judas Priest. On the song "Flotzilla," the band even acknowledged their entry in the Eddie [Iron Maiden]/Vic Rattlehead [Megadeth] mascot sweepstakes—an enormous, mutant lizard.

After the Metallica auditions, Newsted returned to Phoenix to alert friends and family that he'd gotten the gig. Amidst the excitement of joining Metallica, there was a negative side to the deal as well. "I had to tell the Flotsam guys I'd gotten the job. It was really a bitch. There was this thing I used to have posted on the rehearsal-room wall, where I'd listed the 'Seven Points' that should be met when playing; things like Consistency, Concentration, and whatnot. After Eric heard about the Metallica thing, he drew a line through the original seven points, and put a few more up, such as 'Go try out for another band,' all this stuff.

"It was a pretty weird night. In all of a day, I handed everything over. I had piles laid out, of all the fan club stuff, the money and such, and I just handed it over. I went, 'Here you go, man.' They asked their questions about songs; copyrights, and so on, and I gave them all the answers I could. I told them I hoped they understood what I was doing, and to know that I would always be behind them. And I still am behind them, to this day." Newsted's

final gig with Flotsam and Jetsam took place on Halloween night, 1986—exactly five years after his arrival in Arizona.

Metallica backstage with a Japanese fan.

Metallica's first gig with Jason Newsted saw the band take on the unlikely role of opening for Metal Church, under the smaller-than-usual roof of Reseda's Country Club. The secret appearance was announced only to fan club members in the L.A. area via special invitation, but word-of-mouth ensured a quick sellout. The strangely conceived show would see Metallica take an opening position in a modest-sized club at a time when the band was accustomed to headlining coliseums. It made for a more intimate showcase for Jason's string-thumping debut.

Trying to keep his composure, the new bassist sweated bullets backstage, waiting for his call to go on. "At that first gig," recalls Slagel, who had to stand on a table and push out a ceiling panel to see the band through the densely packed crowd, "Jason was the most nervous person I've ever seen in my life! Before the gig, he was terrified. This was his audition—he was in the band, but I think this was one of the last tests he had to pass, and he knew it."

Newsted wasn't the only band member with the jitters. "The whole vibe of that show," reflected Lars in a fan club newsletter, "was that we were *all* so fuckin' nervous! However, in terms of energy, that gig was the most fun we've had in years."

The next night, the band repeated their "surprise opening" strategy during another club gig, this time at Jezabelle's in Anaheim. "It was a hell-hole that held about 300 people, with no room for the equipment," recalls Lars. "It was like looking back on the places we played four years before. People were packed on tables and chairs everywhere, and on the rafters and shit. On the second song of the set, "Master of Puppets," the power went out three times. The only thing that didn't go out was the bass amp, so I just continued playing drums acoustically along with Jason. All the kids were singing. It was brilliant!"

Above: Lars "Trapped Over Ice" in Canada, December, 1986. Opposite: Metalli-Christmas, 1986.

After breaking Jason in live, Metallica hastily made off to Japan on November 12, for a five-date tour. They had contemplated cancelling the tour—they had already cut or changed various European and U.S. dates as a result of the accident—but decided not to, Lars explains, "to pressure us to get our shit together."

For Jason, the Far East dates were a test of his nerves and endurance, as he was forced to withstand the ceaseless, initiation-rite abuse tendered by his bandmates. The "veterans" would frequently jump into a limo and leave him stranded on the curb. Outrageous beverage tabs were charged to his room, often after his bandmates had ripped his door from its hinges. Even autograph sessions would embarrass him: often, after Newsted signed photos with his traditional nickname, "bass face," his mischievous Metallimates would cross out the "b" when the hapless newcomer had his back turned. Thus, Jason became known as "ass face" to legions of Japanese fans!

Japanese culture contrasted heavily with life in America and Europe. "The tour in Japan," recalls Lars, "had different vibes than elsewhere because you don't use buses on the road. Instead, after every gig you stay at a hotel and then travel during the day on a bullet train. Also, there are no support act—ever. You take the stage cold, which is weird, and the shows start early. You get onstage by six and are done by 7:30. In the rest of the world you don't go on any earlier than 9:30!

"In addition to all this, most of the kids in the audience are female. All these twelve-year-old girls follow you around like you're in Bon Jovi or something. I thought Japan was big for bands like Ratt and Motley Crue—bands that relied heavily on the visual end of things. All of a sudden, here were a bunch of 23-year-old ugly fucks like us. But the reception went beyond what any of us had ever dreamed of."

Metallica's scraggly mugs and stripped-down live aura struck such a nerve in Japan that *BURRN!* magazine, the premier Nippon metal bible, voted the band number one in its 1986 reader's poll categories for "Best Group," "Best Live Act," and "Best Song."

✠

After returning home, Metallica played a mini-splurge of sold-out U.S. and Canada dates beginning at New York's Felt Forum in

Lars with comedian Bobcat Goldthwait at The Other Cafe, S.F., 1986.

December and proceeding through Canada and the Northwest. Longtime power-metal peers Metal Church joined them as a support group through the maze of 4,000 to 6,000 seat arenas, which ended in the opening band's hometown of Seattle, Washington, on December 20.

Church bassist Duke Erickson recalls the icy antics that marked their explorations of the Far North: "A lot of the places we played in Canada were hockey rinks. The hockey places would be split in half, with the stage in the middle, and wood over the ice for the kids to stand on. Sometimes, the ice behind the stage would be left open. We'd show up and borrow skates and skate around. I remember playing hockey once and Lars was skating toward me with a hockey stick in his hand. He didn't know how to stop and ended up nailing me in the face. Obviously, our road managers didn't like seeing their bands out trying to learn how to ice skate a half hour before they were to go onstage!"

"We labeled this tour the 'eternal blackness' tour," said Lars in a fan club story, "because the weather was so shitty. It snowed all the time, which caused me to get real sick. I had to sleep with a humidifier on the bus. That was the worst I ever felt on tour. I had a lot of trouble with my lungs—I couldn't really swallow. So when we'd start playing, I'd be coughing, and during the first three songs all this mucus would come out! Flemming, my drum roadie, had a great time cleaning it off my drum kit!"

After Seattle, Metallica took a couple of weeks off. Jason went home to Michigan, Lars to Spain and Morocco, and Kirk and James hung out on Bay Area home turf. In early January, the band met up in Copenhagen, Denmark, for some pre-European tour rehearsals. They passed the time getting drunk on Carlsberg "Christmas beers" and jamming on old NWOBHM favorites by the likes of Diamond Head, Trespass, Angelwitch, and Iron Maiden. Jason, accustomed to the no-nonsense, workmanlike rehearsals he'd had with Flotsam and Jetsam, was flustered by the lack of seriousness. "We had to initiate Jason to the 'Metallica way,'" explains Lars, "meaning that we never want to get too tight. Serious practices might change that!"

Copenhagen represented the starting point of the European tour, but uncomfortable vibes emanated from the Danish city, where this first gig took on a special significance. For Lars, it was a "hometown-boy-makes-good" visit, but more importantly, it was the show which the band had originally set out to play when the bus accident occurred. Jason was faced with the overwhelming task of filling Cliff's shoes. Fortunately, when it came time to play, close to 3,000 roaring freaks greeted Metallica with instantly reassuring open arms. Jason, having gotten over his first-gig jitters, quickly earned the acceptance of the finnicky European crowds with his roaring, rat-a-tat-tat headbanging and distinguished playing.

Winter storms plagued much of the European tour, threatening a reprise of the "eternal darkness" vibe that haunted them in Canada. A gig in Gothenburg, Germany, was cancelled as the most severe winter storm to hit Western Europe in 50 years made roads inaccessible, and the band's equipment truck broke down in the inclement weather.

"Europe in January is too fuckin' cold," remembers Erickson, who along with the rest of his Metal Church bandmates opened the tour. "It was like, 'Let's go sightseeing,' and it's fuckin' 20 below!"

However, Metallica were soon back in form, with memorable jaunts through France and Spain. "It was the first time we'd toured Spain," recalls Lars, "and our first gig, in Barcelona, sold out to over 7,000 people. They're really rowdy in Spain, they fuckin' stormed the merchandise stand when they came in, ripping off hundreds of shirts." Eventually, Metallica made the rounds through Italy before dropping back into Germany and then Zwolle, Holland, for the infamous, much-loved Aardschok festival on February 8.

The festival was the scene of the "Scrap Metal" phenomenon. As Erickson explains it, Scrap Metal was a band comprised of various roadies who had begun doing soundchecks for the bands. During the soundchecks, these crew members began jamming until a fairly tight band had resulted. Lewey, Metal Church's jack-of-all-trades, took on the role of singer, while Metallica roadies Eddie Kercher, Aidan Mullen, and Danny Murphy played bass and twin guitars, respectively. Rounding out the unit was Metallica drum tech Flemming Larsen, who would pound out the beats to a number of cover songs during soundchecks while the merry band of road-dogs-cum-metal-gods surged along with him.

"Peter Mensch thought it was a real funny idea that our roadies had their own band," laughs Duke. "They'd mastered a few cover songs, so Peter set it up so that Scrap Metal would open the Aardschok Festival. Our band members were *their* road crew for that gig. They played in front of 8,000 people, and were nervous as hell. We had one of the other roadies go out in the audience, then jump onstage and attack Lewey, 'cause he was such a charismatic vocal god. They were actually pretty good by then."

Following sets by Crimson Glory, Metal Church, and Anthrax, Metallica threw themselves into their performance, combining the ripping intensity that the fanatical Dutch crowds had come to expect with an almost relaxed, casual humor. By now, the band had adopted what Lars described as "a loose attitude onstage, instead of all this serious bullshit. It was a fun phase, where we'd kinda 'ad lib' on some of the songs—Kirk might chime in with a few bars of a Deep Purple song, then I'd join in and we'd take it from there. The vibe of the last four weeks of the European tour was just tremendous."

Erickson vividly remembers an incident involving Crimson Glory, a Florida-based band whose members fancied wearing chrome masks and costumes onstage. This out-of-place pageantry, made Crimson Glory the brunt of abuse by the other jeans 'n T-shirt metallists on the bill.

"Those guys were hilarious," laughed the Metal Church

bassman. "At the end of the gig, there was a big jam where all the bands got onstage together. The Crimson Glory guys came out in their masks, and they were so pretentious next to the rest of the bands. They had no place being around bands like us." Incensed by their appearance, Hetfield booted one member in the rear, screaming "Get the fuck off our stage!" Crimson Glory, slinking out of sight, quickly obliged.

Metallica, 1987.

En route to the hotel afterwards, Metallica and Metal Church partied together on a single bus. Unfortunately, with poor weather still buffeting the continent, the vehicle broke down on the freeway. To entertain themselves while they were stranded, the army of drunken mates had a cut-out, paste-up session in which Crimson Glory masks were fashioned from paper plates and worn by chuckling members of both bands.

Before their final appearance of the tour, in Sweden, Metallica found themselves with a week's worth of dead space. It proved to be enough time for a jaunt through Poland. "The Poland tour," outlines Lars, "was a lot like the Japan tour in that we were in a new country and didn't know quite what was goin' on. It's tough to get records over there; I must have signed at least seven or eight bootleg copies of *Master of Puppets*. But a lot of the kids really knew all the songs. It was amazing. They really seemed appreciative that we were there."

✠

In early March, Kirk and James rested in San Francisco, with the latter spending most of his time hanging out "at the liquor store." Jason visited family in Phoenix. Lars, however, roamed across Europe and Mexico in typical restless fashion before heading home to the Bay Area. Bored by the sudden lack of activity, he was soon on the phone with the rest of his band, persuading them to enter the rehearsal studio.

Practice sessions were complicated by the reality that the band had moved up in the world. After James and Lars abandoned the infamous 3132 Carlson Boulevard in El Cerrito, the drummer had cozily established himself in a new house up in the hills of Berkeley. The vomit-stained carpets, broken furniture, and comfortably vandalized household at 3132 Carlson had given way to better living conditions, but with this progression went their cherished practice garage. Acting on the assumption that as a bigger band, they ought to try out professional accommodations at a "real" rehearsal studio, the group endured a short-lived stint at a Marin County rehearsal room.

"It was this place with real fancy, up-to-date bullshit," recalled Lars in a fan club interview. "But there was no atmosphere. The people there were real nice and shit, but it wasn't really our kind of scene. We had Night Ranger in one room next to us, and fuckin' Starship in another. The place was fun for about five minutes."

Soon after this unsuccessful attempt to get a more regimented practice routine going, the band suffered another untimely bad "break" when James broke his arm skateboarding for the second time in eight months. This time, the fracture was more serious, requiring some lengthy hospitalization and the immobilization of his arm in a plaster cast. An April appearance on "Saturday Night Live" had to be cancelled, and the band had the opportunity to finish the rest period they'd started before.

"A few things obviously got set back," says Lars. "If we'd started writing new material without James's rhythm guitar, it wouldn't have been too cool a thing, 'cause so much of it is based around the rhythm playing. The rest of us sat around for a while, twiddling our thumbs."

The band solved the rehearsal studio dilemma by customizing Lars's garage. "I had a pretty big two-car garage, after all, the first

Opposite: Kirk with his sizeable collection of comic books and horror film paraphernalia.

three albums were written in a garage, and let's face it, in attitude, anyway, what more are we than a garage band?"

At this point, they were also a garage band with considerably more financial stability. Instead of doing a ramshackle job of modifying their new hangout, the band invested considerable time and money on a professional soundproofing job that went on through the end of May.

In early June, the band began "christening" the garage with a series of extensive jam sessions. To get back into the playing mode, the four plunged into their usual habit of old cover-song rave-ups. Slated for a series of European festival appearances in August, they came up with an idea of releasing an EP of cover songs with a spontaneous, unproduced feel to coincide with the late-summer live dates.

This unorthodox package, which came to be known as *The $5.98 EP—Garage Days Revisited*, followed the "do it different" philosophy which had kept Metallica fresh. From their roots days in L.A., where they jammed fast-paced riffing down the throats of Hollywood glamsters, to their adandonment of thrash in favor of increased dynamic expression on *Ride the Lightning*, to their nose-thumbing at the video medium in favor of an almost underexposed, cultish image, Metallica's emphasis of offering up a different side of the musical coin was once again showcased. "The whole thing on this project," explained Lars, "is not as serious as when we get our own shit together. The vibe is much looser. We were just jamming on a few cover songs, and thought it would be a cool thing to record and release 'em."

The five songs nominated for the EP were "Helpless," by Diamond Head; "The Small Hours" by Blitzkrieg; Killing Joke's "The Wait"; Budgie's "Crash Course In Brain Surgery"; and a "Last Caress/Green Hell" Misfits medley. While the Diamond Head and Blitzkrieg tracks served as Lars's predictable nod to obscure UK metallists, the other songs were selected on the basis of that all-important vibe: that intuitive feel for what was working and what wasn't—not because they were sentimental favorites or early influences. When, during a fan club interview that summer, it was suggested to Lars that the band's choices were somewhat surprising, the drummer appeared to grow defensive: "Isn't that the whole integrity of this fuckin' band to do different shit? We've always tried to avoid following what everyone else is doing. It's a challenge to come up with things that are original. It's not easy, but that's part of the fun."

The search for a studio to record the EP wasn't exactly fun.

Kirk Hammett in a surprise appearance on Anthrax's "Among the Living" tour, Santa Monica, 1986.

During the summer of 1985, when Lars and James had gone studio-hunting in LA for a decent haunt to record *Master of Puppets*, they discovered only one they deemed suitable: Conway Studios. Unfortunately, the popular facility wasn't available. While the band had to make due with Copenhagen's reliable Sweet Silence studios for that record, they continued to keep Conway in mind. Now they hoped to use the studio to record the EP, but were dismayed to find that Ted Nugent had booked up time there and was hard at work recording his new album.

But fate intervened. "Burnstein and Mensch used to manage Nugent. So somehow, someone, somewhere, convinced Ted to take five or six days off around Independence Day. So old Ted fuckin' hung up his guitar for a few days and let Metallica come in and create chaos."

With songs and studio in hand, the band now set out in search of the final piece of their EP puzzle: an engineer. Two people were available at Conway: one had produced a few metal-oriented albums, but the other was a jazz/fusion and country/western veteran. In characteristic "go-against-the-grain" tradition, Metallica chose the latter. "We ended up with an engineer who had never been near a heavy metal band. It made things interesting."

It took Metallica less than four weeks to conceptualize, rehearse, and record *The $5.98 EP*, a fraction of the time spent on *Master of Puppets*. The in-and-out pace, the relaxed, unproduced strategy, and the unusual concept and song selections made the EP a "fan oriented" item—an "acquired taste" disc that even the band admitted might not be for everyone.

It did not, however, prevent the EP from going gold on the album charts in less than six weeeks, spawning countless imitations. Its no-frills sleeve notes, sparse and handwritten by James, was among the features that suddenly made it "cool" for bands to pump out between-album EPs with minimalist production and packaging. Metallica's "warts and all" approach saw them include an out-of-tune introduction to Iron Maiden's hokey "Run to the Hills" during the EP's final fadeout, demonstrating that they hadn't lost their sense of humor.

Ulrich had something else cooking, a visual companion piece to *Garage Days* that would double as a tribute to the memory of Cliff Burton. "Tribute" wasn't a word the band liked to throw around—Cliff's death had to date been treated in a respectfully low-key way. But to Lars, a video compilation that exclusively featured footage of the Burton-era band seemed a perfect homage.

The resulting home video, Metallica's first, was dubbed *Cliff 'em*

All. "Instead of doing the typical nine-camera, super-duty phonic sound thing, with fuckin' super-stereo this, that, and the other thing, we thought of a different approach," explained Lars during the video's pre-production. "There are a lot of bootleg recordings out there of Metallica. We thought, why not get these for everyone so that people can buy them together, instead of getting some 15th generation shit tape from a tape trader."

The tape begins with the band entering a grocery store to buy beer. Then the clips shoot by, with footage as old as Cliff's second gig with the band, in March 1983, and as recent as the Ozzy tour three years later. Some of the snippets are professionally shot, like a crisp MTV segment filmed during the band's first "Day on the Green" show in Oakland and a "Metal Hammer Festival" rave-up from Euro-television. Others are wobbly, grainy bits shot by fans.

"Some of it is real primitive," admitted Lars, explaining that the crudeness was intentional. "It's something that the whole band felt was cool, 'cause the way a typical kid in the audience sees a show is similar to these one-camera bootlegs, zooming in on whoever in the band he wants to, then fuckin' banging a little bit so the thing's a little bit out of focus. And when some fuckin' drunk guy next to him falls into him, for five seconds you see a bit of the ceiling or a bit of the chair he's sitting on. That kind of thing makes for a really cool vibe. It's hella-Metallica."

Ad for 1987 "Monsters of Rock" festival in the UK.

On the eve of *The $5.98 EP*'s release, Metallica ravaged the Castle Donington stage for the second time. Things had changed since their appearance two years earlier, when the music had almost taken a backseat to the fascinating assortment of stage-aimed projectiles. On that occasion the band had also been unflatteringly positioned in the nether regions of the bill. On this August 22, evening, however, Metallica was second only to Bon Jovi, whose headlining status had to be expected, considering that their ultra-slick, hyper-glossy megahit album *Slippery When Wet* was the current international "flavor of the month." Metallica, on the other hand, had only their bizarre, covers-only EP to present. However, their name brought swarms of disciples to honor them.

With this in mind, the band took to the road on "The Monsters of Rock" tour, a live stadium assault through 23 U.S. cities headlined by Van Halen. Several support groups, including Scorpions, Dokken, and Kingdom Come, trailed the good-time, party-rock headliners; Metallica was sandwiched somewhere in between, fourth on the bill.

The huge festival, which ran for several weeks, with the five bands playing in sequence, got its official start on May 27, 1988, in East Troy, Wisconsin, where the bands kicked off the extravaganza before a crowd of 40,000 people. Metallica, billed as "Frayed Ends," surprised Southern California fans days earlier with an unannounced appearance at L.A.'s Troubador. The band still hadn't lost their taste for intimate club gigs, a taste the stadium-sized "Monsters..." shows, which would continue through August 1, certainly couldn't satisfy.

Although the "Monsters..." tour would be pronounced a finan-

cial failure—presumably due to a poor economy and the 10-hour-plus endurance marathon the shows subjected listeners to—it gave Metallica an opportunity to expose themselves to legions of previously uninitiated arena-rock fans. As on previous festival bills, Metallica stuck out like a sore thumb, which was of course, to their advantage. "We're the underdogs," commented Kirk to *New York Times* rock critic Jon Pareles. "We haven't had a Top 10 hit, and we look like a bunch of bums out there. Amidst all this glam and this huge production, we're going to stick out. But that's what we're here for—and that's what put us here in the first place."

Backstage with Van Halen on 1988 U.S. "Monsters of Rock" tour.

IN SEARCH OF THE NEW!

CHAPTER 6

AFTER METALLICA'S LATEST bit of road-roaming, the quest for new music became a top priority. The band was psyched to inject some in-studio blood into their recording routine, and Mike Clink, who'd transformed himself from a reliable engineer of UFO albums to the "producer of the hour" after his work on Guns N' Roses' gigantic debut album *Appetite for Destruction,* seemed like the right guy. Band and producer recorded two rough cover tracks of Budgie's "Breadfan" and Diamond Head's "The Prince," and began work on drum tracks to two new cuts, "Harvester of Sorrow" and "The Shortest Straw."

However, Clink didn't click. The band, unhappy with the sounds that emerged from their collaboration, soon dismissed him and called upon engineer Flemming Rasmussen. On January 29, the tried and true "Metalli-Rasmussen" chemistry was conjured up for four months in the posh confines of L.A.'s One On One studio. In early May, *...And Justice for All* was wrapped and soon surfaced as the fourth Metallica album.

While most hard-rock or metal bands seem to reach an artistic peak with their third albums, after which they submerge into either self-imitation or tired, passive, "we're rich now, so why bother?" indifference, Metallica took their angriest, least commercial stance to date with *...Justice.* Their success was a fact, and their pocketbooks

---

Opposite: Metallica in Oakland before performing at October 15th's "Day on the Green," 1991.

bulged thick with green. Such comforts, one would assume, would diffuse the angry, punkish vibe that had given the band's past releases their edge. So, it was surprising when ...*Justice* screamed its scathing critique of American hypocrisy with its pulsating audio visions of a world held hostage by the claws of fear, lies, and greed. Just as *Ride the Lightning* emerged as a dark primer on death, and *Master of Puppets* explored manipulation of the masses, Metallica's latest gave the finger to anything that was left. With a production as sparse as its lyrical deathscapes of blistered earth ("Blackened") and battlefield mutilation ("One"), the album was no easy listen. Its relative inaccessibility was enhanced further by the lengthy, progressive, stop-start vibe of the songs. The title track and "To Live Is to Die," another building instrumental in the spirit of "...Ktulu" or "Orion," both clocked in just short of 10 minutes each.

With nary a light moment anywhere within earshot, ...*Justice* took on blacklisting in "The Shortest Straw," a dysfunctional, greed-based legal system in "...And Justice for All," censorship in "Eye of The Beholder," grief in "Harvester of Sorrow," and the generation gap in "Dyers Eve," a manic track that explored another side of "Fade to Black's" fatalistic, end-it-all tone. While the latter song seemed resigned and placid, "Dyers Eve" howled its rage in the form of an anguished suicide letter:

> *Dear mother*
> *Dear father*
> *Hidden in your world you've made for me*
> *I'm seething*
> *I'm bleeding*
> *Ripping wounds in me that never heal*
> *Undying spite I feel for you*
> *Living out this hell you always knew*

As though the light-speed jumps already made by Metallica were merely pathetic warm-up events, the band's course of action became even faster as they jetted into the new decade. "Like Luke Skywalker blasting the death star into oblivion," observed Seattle's *Rocket* magazine, "the force is definitely with this band." And with the huge exception of Cliff's untimely death, it did seem as though some inherent, omniscient sixth sense was guiding the band through all the right hoops. They were at the top of their genre, and it appeared they wouldn't just maintain this majestic position into the Nineties, but would transcend it.

Opposite: Lars Ulrich in Burbank strip bar, May 1991.

The first step toward attaining this heavy metallized immortality was a grueling, 16-month tour of the world to promote the *...And Justice for All* album. The "Damaged Justice Tour" would take the conquering heroes into such previously uncharted realms as New Zealand and Australia. Opening in Budapest, Hungary, on September 11, 1988, the global trek posed an interesting challenge. It couldn't be denied that at this stage in their career, the

Kirk with Kim Thayil of
Soundgarden, October 1991.

band was an "arena act." This meant theatrics. It meant lighting rig assemblies careening every which way, blasting laser beams in a flourescent techno-dance that rivaled an end-of-the-world duel between robotic terminators in a James Cameron film. It meant choreography. It meant costumes. It meant...er, none of the above. On the contrary, Metallica shuddered at the thought of being sucked into the "biggest-brightest-loudest" vacuum that swept bands like Kiss and Iron Maiden away, with their fire-breathing theatrics and towering, oversized monster mascots lurching across the stage. How could Metallica balance the street integrity they'd worked hard to maintain with a "more-for-your-money" stage show that fans would demand?

They eventually compromised with a live atmosphere that

centered around the "scales of justice" theme: Lady Justice, dilapidated, cracked and impotent, teetered in statue form behind Lars's high-perched drums, with Roman pillars and marble blocks scattered about. Such imagery, sparse by the standards of most stage productions, would be the closest Metallica would come to a theatrical presentation. If fans were disappointed with the lack of guitar-smashing and flying confetti, they'd eventually be won over by Metallica's 2 1/2 hour set and provocative opening slots by such bands as Danzig, The Cult, Queensryche, and Faith No More.

Meanwhile, their album would sell an unprecedented number of units, peaking at number six on the U.S. charts on October 9. Singles, another relatively untapped area for the band, followed suit, and "Eye of the Beholder," "Harvester of Sorrow," and "One" all scored minor hits. The latter track would be further immortalized in Metallica's first video, shot on December 6, which intercut footage of the band playing in an isolated L.A. warehouse with scenes of the Dalton Trumbo cult classic *Johnny Got His Gun*. The film tells the tale of a mortally wounded soldier whose ability to communicate is all but snuffed out when he ventures onto a minefield and is blown into an expressionless stump. He remained a living brain, doomed to sensory-deprivation. The song is "Trapped Under Ice" all over again, with Hetfield's horrifying chant accenting the claustrophobic, urgent tone of the song:

Darkness
Imprisoning me
I cannot see
Absolute horror
I cannot live
I cannot die
Trapped in myself
body my holding cell;
Landmine
Has taken my sight
Taken my speech
Taken my hearing
Taken my arms
Taken my legs
Taken my soul
Left me with life in hell!

"One," fueled by its potent black and white video and gradual, acoustic-to-all-out-speed-metal format, made it the band's first bona-fide hit, and the "Stairway to Heaven" of the cynical, death-obsessed Eighties. On January 10, 1989, it was released as a single which eventually peaked at number 35 on the U.S. charts.

It also served as Metallica's showcase at their first appearance—indeed, the first appearance ever by any metal band—at the prestigious Grammy Awards. Now, anyone who has been exposed to any western culture at all knows that a 4,000-member panel of music industry voters annually determine the Grammy nominations and winners in a number of categories spanning all genres of modern music. The Thirty-First Annual Grammy show, held on February 22, 1989, marked the first time in which the panel included a "Best Metal Performance" among the categories. The denim 'n leather carpet was rolled out for Metallica, who with their performance, represented the newly recognized genre before thousands of tuxedo-clad musical bureacrats. There was something supremely twisted and off-kilter about seeing the innocuous, well-manicured Billy Crystal introducing "Metalllicaaaa!" to the polite assembly. At first, the band's sound was sub-standard and James's voice quivered noticeably, but by the time Metallica blasted "One's" final rat-ta-tat riffs, the music had knocked the cobwebs from the rafters of L.A.'s Shrine Auditorium. Just another unlikely triumph for James, Lars, and company.

Later in the program, Alice Cooper and Lita Ford approached the podium to announce the winner of the "Best Metal Performance" category. Along with Metallica, the nominees included Jane's Addiction, Jethro Tull, Iggy Pop, and AC/DC. Though Metallica seemed to strike everyone and his mother as an easy shoo-in to win, the honors instead went to Tull, mid-Seventies has-beens. This band was best remembered not for their raging riffs but the petite, flute-wielding singer Ian Anderson, who delivered onstage ramblings about "Puppies, red and rosey" and beasts 'n broadswords while perched upon one leg. Upon opening the envelope and seeing the winner, Lita Ford stifled a laugh.

As the televised broadcast cut to a commercial, a cascade of boos swept the packed pavillion.

✠

The Grammies ushered in the era of "Industry Recognition/Awards" for Metallica. At MTV's 1989 Music Awards show, Metallica was nominated for best video with "One," but were beaten out by Guns N' Roses' huge "Sweet Child O' Mine." In a show of respect and spiritual camaraderie, Guns' bassist Duff McKagan said in his acceptance speech that he felt Metallica had truly deserved the honor. The New Music Awards, another tele

Opposite: James on stage, "Wherever I May Roam" tour, 1991.

vised, "post-Grammies" presentation, honored Metallica with a "Best Metal Album" award.

These ceremonies filled the time gaps of the "Damaged Justice" tour, which concluded in Sao Paulo, Brazil, on October 8. Metallica had dished up over 250 performances, every one a physical challenge and a magical exchange of power between fans and band. Rather than take a well-deserved hybernation, however, the band took on projects in characteristic, keep-on-movin' spirit.

Ulrich, for instance, tore into a compilation album venture that had obsessed him for years. The story behind the creation of *New Wave Of British Heavy Metal: '79 Revisited*, is told by both Lars and Geoff Barton, the influential British journalist/editor for *Sounds* newspaper and *Kerrang!* magazine. In the album's liner notes, Barton explained that brainstorming for the vintage metal collection took place when he and Lars were assembling a Metallica tour book. They spoke of the fact that the 10-year anniversary of the glorious burst of independent Brit bands which had inspired and preoccupied the Metallica drummer was approaching. Lars, utterly amazed that 10 years had actually gone by, insisted that the two nostalgia-soaked NWOBHM experts should collaborate on a commemorative album.

James Hetfield, 1991.

Barton immortalized the moment on the sleeve notes: "My heart sinks, but Lars is on a roll. 'Diamond Head! Witchfynder General! Vardis! Praying Mantis!' he shrieks. 'Dragster! Fist! Sledgehammer! Jaguar!' I respond as Lars's enthusiasm becomes suddenly, stupidly infectious."

After the team compiled a list of various choice NWOBHM bands and their best songs, *New Wave...* was well on its way up the audio birth canal, its creators preparing for the delivery in the manner of two expectant fathers setting up a nursery. England's Phonogram Records agreed to release the disc overseas, but Lars delegated U.S. distribution to Slagel's Metal Blade label. Aware that the indie-label kingpin was as big a fan of that musical era as he was, Ulrich knew Slagel would accord it the attention it deserved. But there were other problems.

"The project wasn't as easy as Lars had expected it to be," remembers Slagel. "He had a lot of problems. I think he felt he would get a band listing together and give it to the people at Phonogram, but it wasn't that easy. Finding some of these people was very difficult for them. [To locate some such long-lost musicians, Lars would turn in desperation to the London phone book, and call all the numbers listed for a certain name and ask, "Are you the guy who used to play in Holocaust?" or "Were you once the guitarist for Angel Witch?" and so on.] Some of the bands even had an attitude about being on the record. You would think that you'd find this band that existed 10 years ago to be very happy to lend their songs, but a lot of these groups had gone through tough periods, or they don't wanna remember what they did, or the guys in the band all hated each other—that kind of crap. What began as a fun project became a nightmare."

A matter concerning the record's cover photo was but one of a myriad of obstacles the drummer-turned-producer was forced to

Metallica with legendary concert promoter Bill Graham, October 1991.

hurdle. "The record was about ready to come out in Europe," continues Slagel, "and at the last minute, the guy who owns Polygram nixed the cover. The cover featured Thunderstick, the drummer from Samson, who wore a mask. The PolyGram guy said it looked too much like a rapist who had done a bunch of horrible things in England 10 years ago. They didn't want that association, so they moved a bunch of other pictures to hide his face. We put out the original cover in America, which Lars appreciated."

New Wave... finally saw the light of day in the fall of 1990. It's an indispensable slab of vinyl for any serious Metallica fan, primarily because it reveals those raw, vital tidbits of U.K. ear-candy that so profoundly influenced the trademark energetic riffing that Metallica came to perfect and popularize many years later. The guitar backbones that dominate Holocaust's "Death Or Glory," or Angel Witch's "Extermination Day," for instance, would be right at home on *Kill 'em All*. In fact, Metallica seemed to have stolen some of the era's better moments for themselves: "Seek and Destroy" blatantly lifts its riff from Diamond Head's "Dead Reckoning" (which isn't on the compilation, but can be found on a single by the persistent collector), and "For Whom the Bell Tolls" swipes from the Angel Witch cut, "Angel of Death" (from the album *Angel Witch* on Bronze Records). The record admirably places a by-gone era in a time capsule.

✠

1990 saw Metallica sprint off the starting blocks and into the studio to record a slapdash cover version of Queen's "Stone Cold Crazy." The recording served as the band's contribution to *Rubaiyat*, a compilation album commemorating the 40th anniversary of Elektra Records, which featured several of the label's acts covering songs by other Elektra artists. It was an ambitous, daring concept that seemed in spirit with the Ulrichian "do something different!" philosophy. The bare-bones recording was a throwback to the primitive method and sound of *The $5.98 EP*, and was an effective rendition of one of Freddy Mercury's heaviest songs ever.

✠

In February, as if to apologize for the Jethro Tull episode, the NARASS organization awarded Metallica with a "Best Metal Performance" Grammy for their "One" single. Once more, the group had refused to pander to the industry, preferring to wait until the industry came to them.

✠

Summer had become synonymous with festivals for Metallica, what with their memories of Donningtons and "Day on the Greens" past, and 1990 was no exception. A cluster of European one-offs was followed by open-air dates with Aerosmith across the East Coast and through Canada. But the instinct to write new material and father another in-studio baby soon took over. Unhappy with the lengthy, ultra-progressive style of *...And Justice for All*, the band opted for a songwriting style based on stripped-down, basic rhythms. This approach, pumped up by producer Bob Rock, was the foundation of Metallica's fifth, self-titled album.

The band's choice of Rock as a producer provoked a fan response reminiscent of the pre-*Ride the Lightning* hysteria over

Metallica, 1989.

"Fade to Black." The band was forced to endure rumors that the new album would abandon their time-honored style of militant metal mania in favor of the glossy sound with which their new producer imbued such recent commercial pop albums as Bon Jovi's *Slippery When Wet* and Motley Crue's *Dr. Feelgood*. But Lars, who spent his backstage "Damaged Justice" tour spells humming "Dr. Feelgood" in appreciative honor of a band he'd once provoked in Los Angeles for being unredeemable posers, admired Rock's craftsmanship on the latest Crue opus. Indeed, Rock had a great ear for definition and polish, and his collaboration with heavier bands like The Cult had resulted in brilliant hard-rock gusto delivered to technical perfection. Even the notorious Led Zeppelin ripoffs Kingdom Come scored a hit with their debut album under Rock's studio guidance. Still, the sell-out rumors persisted.

On October 6, sessions began at L.A.'s One On One studio for *Metallica*. The album, which was concluded in June 1991, was introduced to the world via a band-hosted record-release party at New York's Madison Square Garden on August 3, 1991. Ten thousand gathered for the free-of-charge affair, at which all four group members nervously slinked through the crowd, monitoring its response to the music blasting from the P.A. system.

Despite its exploration of new soundscapes and uncharacteristic styles, the album won the masses over easily. "Enter Sandman," *Metallica*'s opening track, actually contained something resembling a catchy hook in its anchoring riff; "Sad But True" was a grinding dirge classic which tread the mid-Seventies ground of Led Zeppelin and Black Sabbath; and "The Unforgiven" was made memorable by a huge-sounding verse and subtle choruses (a combination that contrasted with the quiet-verse, heavy-chorus formula of previous Metallitunes like "One" and "Fade to Black"). Fast, pounding tracks like "Holier Than Thou," "Through the Never," and "The Struggle Within" moved along frantically, but without the throwaway bridges and multiple time changes that marked previous high-energy compositions.

"Don't Tread on Me" was a patriotic anthem falsely construed as a "pro-Gulf War" statement by left-wing critics the world over, causing considerable media flack that left the band in disgusted disbelief. It seemed a laughable irony that a positive, pro-America statement (completely unheard of in any of rock's authority-hating, anarchistic genres) would be savaged by such high-profile journals as *Rolling Stone* and even *Playboy*. After churning out four records of cynical despair, Metallica was now taking it up the backside for expressing even four minutes of faith and optimism.

Other surprises abounded on *Metallica*. A sitar introduced the atmospheric road tune "Wherever I May Roam"; "The God That Failed" explored Hetfield's distaste for the Christian Science doctrines he was raised to accept during his dark adolescence in Downey; and "My Friend of Misery" was a bass-driven condemnation of agitators and "whiners" that seemed perfectly tailored for the anti- "Don't Tread on Me" crowd.

Meanwhile, "Nothing Else Matters" emerged as the most personal song Metallica had ever recorded, a ballad of classic proportions. With its Michael Kamen-orchestrated backing arrangement and no sign of the violent, climactic "storm-after-the-calm" amplification that had marked previous Metallica ballads, the song appeared to be a testimonial to the band's accomplishments and personal growth. The lyrics of "Nothing Else Matters"' seem at first glance to be those of a standard love song, but their vague tone suggest less a romantic affection than a love of camaraderie and the power of fulfilled trust:

Opposite: James at L.A.'s One On One recording studio, February 1991.

Never opened myself this way
Life is ours, we live it our way
All these words I don't just say
And nothing else matters

Trust I seek and I find in you
Every day for us something new
Open mind for a different view
And nothing else matters.

Metallica was a landmark album that one-upped the band's past achievements on nearly every level. Rock's production was seamless, Hammett's leads took on a tasty, blues-based dimension, and Hetfield's vocals and lyrical abilities topped anything he'd done before. The disc leaped to number one on the U.S. charts with its release on August 12.

Then there was the cover. In the spirit of Led Zeppelin's vague sleeve artwork, as well as the minimalist feel of *The $5.98 EP* and *Cliff 'em All* video, both of which featured scribbled sleeve notes and underplayed packaging, Metallica opted for a cover of solid black, on which only the subtle outline of the band's logo and the shape of a "Don't Tread on Me" flag-serpent appear. The snake took on an eerie identity of its own, like Zep's *Zoso* symbols or the lips-and-tongue logo of The Rolling Stones.

And there were plenty of hits, including "Enter Sandman," which rose to the Top 20 on the U.S. charts, "The Unforgiven," "Nothing Else Matters," "Wherever I May Roam," and "Sad But True." The band's five-barreled singles assault spawned videos, which regularly topped MTV's weekend "Headbanger's Ball" program and established a wider fan bass for Metallica.

And then there were the ensuing live coups, each bigger and more memorable than the last: On August 17, 1991, Metallica played second on the bill at yet another "Monsters of Rock" festival at Castle Donington, in a group lineup that also included the Black Crowes, Queensryche, Motley Crue, and headliners AC/DC; there was their early September appearance on MTV's 1991 Music Awards show, where they played a roaring rendition of "Enter Sandman" but unfortunately lost the "Best Heavy Metal Band" award to Aerosmith; a revolutionary festival in Moscow, Russia, which attracted 500,000 fans, where the band played in a historic musical *tour de force* that commemorated the country's conversion from communism to democracy. The huge outdoor one-off, taking place on September 28, at Moscow's Tushino Airfield, also featured AC/DC, The Black Crowes, and Pantera, and should have been a peaceful expression of newfound freedom and peace, but the brutal intervention of Soviet police left 53 people injured.

Live milestones just kept on coming. On October 12, Metallica began their juggernaut "Wherever I May Roam" tour, which featured a diamond-shaped stage setup making it possible for audiences to see the band from all four sides of an arena. Def Leppard had pulled a similar stage concept off on their recent "Hysteria" road trek, but Metallica chiseled the idea into a customized, original design featuring a hollowed-out "snake pit" center in which select members of the press and fortunate fans could gawk at the band from a more intimate perspective.

Meanwhile, the tour had hardly gotten underway when the band snuck home to headline a "Day on the Green" festival at the Oakland Stadium that also featured Queensryche, Faith No More, and Soundgarden. A sad footnote to Metallica's D.O.G. legacy, which saw them go from fourth on the bill in 1985 to headlining the show in front of 50,000 hometown fans, was the death of festival promoter Bill Graham in a helicopter crash shortly after the October 15 show.

Another tour break was filled by a second Grammy performance on February 25, 1992, in where they played "Enter Sandman." They were nominated for "Best Heavy Metal Performance," and despite facing heavy, legitimate competition from Megadeth, Anthrax, Motorhead, and Soundgarden, they won the Grammy. They accepted their overdue award with barbed tongues firmly planted in cheeks. "I think the first thing we've gotta do is thank Jethro Tull for not putting out an album this year," announced Lars to the howling Grammy audience. "Also, we've gotta thank the Academy for giving Jethro Tull the award in 1989: read between the lines, know what I mean?"

After offering the band's obligatory thanks to Bob Rock, Q-Prime management, and Elektra, Lars concluded with cocky sarcasm: "I wanna thank all the radio stations and MTV, without whom all of this was possible anyway! Just kidding...."

Metallica had now chalked up three Grammy victories, demonstrated their supremacy as a critical darling and respected industry monument. No metal band before them—not Aerosmith, not Black Sabbath, not even Led Zeppelin— had managed to fill their trophy cases and move albums with such rapidity.

With their latest record reaching quadruple platinum status, Grammies piling up on their fireplace mantels, and live shows continuing to sell out around the world, Metallica had become the biggest metal-genre entity in existence. No band of even a hard rock persuasion seemed to near the peak that Metallica had climbed to, except, perhaps, for the controversial L.A. supergroup Guns N' Roses. Thus, when the death of Queen's Freddie Mercury from his affliction with AIDS prompted a multi-artist fundraiser in

Great Britain called "A Concert for Life," both bands jumped onto the bill in a "dream team" duo that had metal fans glued to their television sets during its April 20, 1992 airing. Metallica's short set, which opened a day-long celebrity curtain call featuring such diverse rock legends as Elton John, David Bowie, and Def Leppard, included "Enter Sandman," "Sad But True," and "Nothing Else Matters." The concert's climactic heavy-rock peak, however, came in the form of "Stone Cold Crazy," backed up by the guitar/drum/bass trio of Queen survivors Brian May, Roger Taylor, and John Deacon, and featuring Black Sabbath's Tony Iommi on rhythm

Lars and Kirk on band tour plane, 1991.

guitar and Hetfield on vocals. The sight of riff-inventor Iommi, who'd first brought doomy downpicking into fashion on such early Sabbath records as *Paranoid* and *Sabotage*, sharing the Wembley Stadium stage with Hetfield, guitar's contemporary rhythm king, brought tears of adulation and pleasant disbelief to the eyes of onlooking metal afficionados.

Soon afterwards, Metallica would once again stand aside the awards podium to collect a "Best Metal Video" statue for "Enter Sandman" at MTV's 1992 awards broadcast.

After their headlining tour was wrapped up in the mid-summer

of 1982, Metallica would again share the stage with Guns N' Roses during one of the most ambitious stadium bills in history: in a package that had been researched and organized since February, both bands agreed to co-headline a 24-date tour through America's larger cities. With a format reminiscent of the 1988 "Monsters of Rock" tour, in which the two powerhouses and openers Faith No More would combine sets for over seven hours of straight music per show, the tour kicked off at Washington, D.C.'s RFK Stadium to 50,000 fans. Things went smoothly until the Guns' charismatic and controversial frontman Axl Rose suffered throat problems that resulted in mid-tour cancellations. For Metallica, however, the tour's biggest glitch would come during an August 9th performance at Montreal, Canada's Olympic Stadium, in which Hetfield walked into a flashpot and suffered second-degree burns on his face, arms, hands, and legs. At the time of this writing, Hetfield is recovering at a Denver burn clinic, and reports announcing his progress are encouraging.

Lars on stage during "Wherever I May Roam," tour, 1991.

✠

What dramatic last words can be uttered about Metallica? What kind of climactic statement would summarize and do justice to the

band? None. A brown-nosing, last-words appraisal simply wouldn't fit a group whose very essence and appeal stem from the fact that the Metalliguys are just plain...people. They pursued what they enjoyed doing most. They wrestled with issues of compatibility and direction. They got their efforts across to others by any means available, starving and struggling along the way. They suffered through tragedies and broadened their potential. And they just so happened to get very famous along the way. Aside from the fame bit, these qualities put them on common ground with every human being that has ever walked the earth. Here's hoping the Metallica story encourages those who hear it to strive for the same creative, courageous, and persistent heights in their own lives.

Opposite: At Oakland after "Day on the Green" gig, October 15, 1991. Below: Appeasing the masses, 1991.

TALES FROM THE "TRUES"

CHAPTER 7

THERE IS AN early Metallica interview in which the band, between swigs of vodka, yell out their anger at the fact that an uninspired L.A. band has stolen an old Budgie riff for one of their songs. Their rage clearly expresses Metallica's conviction that this bit of musical plagiarism is unforgivable. The interviewer reasons that the band probably figured that no one would remember the Budgie song, and assumed that they could get away with the sneaky theft.

Hetfield, pausing to ponder this, loudly proclaims, "Yeah, but the 'trues' would know! They'd remember!"

The drunken frontman's term refers to those true, old-guard headbangers whose heavy metal dues were paid through an adolescence of record-buying sprees and studious, rock 'n roll research. The "trues," James emphasizes, would be the first to squawk when a number as truly classic as "Breadfan" shows up as a substandard rehash done by some wannabe L.A. glam band.

The term might also serve to distinguish veteran Metallibangers—those who salivated while waiting for the postman to deliver that eagerly anticipated "No Life 'til Leather" demo from a gracious pen pal, or furiously grappled through a sea of tight-knit bodies to get to the front of the stage for an Old Waldorf Metalligig in Frisco—from those who, 10 years later, succumbed to the

Opposite: James at The Stone, San Franciso,
March 5th 1983

band's overwhelming popularity and finally bought an album as a symbolic and pathetic gesture of conforming "hipness."

Brian Lew and Ron Quintana are textbook examples of "trues." The former immediately befriended the band after admiring their demos and beholding their first Bay Area gigs; Brian was front and center during those frothy, rude shows, bobbing his head and taking timeless photos. And his *Whiplash* fanzine was considered one of the best underground metal 'zines of its time. Quintana, with his legendary University of San Francisco "Rampage Radio" show and witty, informative, tongue-in-cheek fan magazine *Metal Mania*, served as San Francisco's metal guru.

Lew is low-key and understated, but his mind is loaded with facts and figures related to alternative music and popular culture. His current fanzine, *Umlaut*, is a free-form journal of essays on topics ranging from the pomposity of Morrissey to the absurdity of contemporary toys. (He cites the Playdough food factory, which allows children to change clammy, fluorescent puddles of putty-like gunk into the shape of hamburgers, hot dogs, and other fast food items, as a particularly repulsive offender). Quintana, meanwhile, sports waist-long hair, flannel shirts, and confesses to a love of campy television icons like "The Brady Bunch" and "Mr. Rogers." His Haight-Ashbury flat features a kitchen ceiling webbed in pink silly-string, from which assorted dolls and rubber toys dangle lifelessly.

In the pages that follow, both longtime Metallica experts give their respective views on how they met the band, how Metallica's music changed the course of metal music, and how they interpret the band's success. While some of the times, places, and events have already been touched on, the "trues" perspectives, peppered with personal anecdotes and memories, add a three-dimensional scope to the facts; they also provide further keys to what makes Metallica's music so contagious, exciting, and memorable.

Kirk jamming with Primus at The Omni, S.F., 1990.

THE BAY AREA
CLUB DAYS REVISITED
By Brian Lew

IN THE EARLY 1980s, the main Bay Area concert clubs were The Old Waldorf and the three Keystone clubs in San Francisco, Berkeley, and Palo Alto. The Waldorf was the premier venue for years until it closed in July 1983. The Keystone circuit sometimes made it possible to see a band three times, because the performers were usually booked at all three clubs. The Keystone Berkeley closed in 1985; the Palo Alto club shut its doors in 1986.

Early in 1982 the magazine *Kerrang!* showed up at a local record store. I began buying it religiously, along with the weekly English hard rock paper *Sounds*. Through the pen pals and letters section in *Kerrang!,* I became friends with K.J. Doughton, Ron Quintana, and other Heavy Metal tape traders in the U.S., Canada,

England, and Holland. In September 1982, a Metal Blade Records show was scheduled for The Stone in San Francisco, to coincide with the release of their first *Metal Massacre* compilation. The bill included Bitch and Cirith Ungol, but four days before the show Cirith Ungol cancelled and Metallica replaced them. K.J. had sent me their "No Life 'til Leather" demo over the summer, and it immediately became a fixture in my tape player. When K.J. called to tell me Metallica had replaced Cirith Ungol I was very psyched, and dragged as many friends with me to The Stone as I could. A couple of days before the show I called Dave Mustaine in L.A. to make arrangements to meet the band once they got to San Francisco. We met in front of the club, where Lars's green Pacer (with white interior!) hitched to a U-haul trailer, was parked. I reviewed the evening's performance in *Northwest Metal* #2.

First photo session with Cliff in El Cerrito, January 1983.

METALLICA
The Stone, San Francisco
September 18, 1982

This was the night! The heaviest band in the U.S. of A., Metallica, rampaged into the City By The Bay and spread more havoc than the 1906 earthquake!

Due to poor publicity, The Stone was only half full. However, a small contingent of Metallica fans were on hand to do some serious headbanging to the tune of "The Young Metal Attack." We weren't disappointed.

Despite being stopped earlier in the evening by the S.F.P.D. for carrying open cans of brew on the street, Metallica took the stage at 10:30 sharp and immediately slammed into "Hit the Lights," and the headbanging commenced! Next came the spine-cracker "The Mechanix," and the dark onslaught of "Phantom Lord."

Their sheer intensity was incredible! Fusing the pile driving madness of Motorhead and Venom with their own insanity, the band devastated their audience with a non-stop, fast, and ultra-furious set of Heavy Metal. The superb rhythm section of Lars Ulrich (drums) and Ron McGovney (bass) set the neck-breaking pace, while the searing leads of Dave Mustaine and the rhythm work and outrageous vocals of James Hetfield set the mood.

Following a chorus of requests, the group ripped into the fiery inferno of "Jump in the Fire," and slowed things down to Mach 10, for the love song, "Motorbreath." Next, they showcased a new song "No Remorse," that shook the dust from the rafters. Following came the firestorm "Seek and Destroy," and closing the regular set was the ode to rivetheads everywhere, "Metal Militia."

The already hoarse headbangers down front demanded more and were rewarded with fantastic versions of two Diamond Head songs, "Am I Evil" and "The Prince." At that point, unfortunately, Metallica had to relinquish the stage.

✠

After the show, Metallica sold their short-lived "Young Metal Attack" shirts. Band

Cliff, Halloween, 1983, Palo Alto, CA.

and crew were lodging at a dilapidated hotel two blocks from The Stone called Sam Wong's, and once back there commenced drinking, signing autographs, and posing for photos. Metallica had been officially introduced to San Francisco.

The Stone, San Francisco, March 19, 1983.

A month later, the band returned to play a Metal Monday at The Old Waldorf on Battery Street (these early days at the Waldorf were immortalized in the song "Battery," on *Master of Puppets*). My friends and I met them as they arrived at the club and helped load-in their equipment. We were then passed off as crew members so we could stay for the soundcheck. By coincidence, the date was on October 18, 1982, my 19th birthday. I asked if the show could be taped for me, so they plugged their tape player into the mixing board. After the show, Mustaine was so unhappy with their performance that he didn't want me to have the tape; he even threatened to destroy it (he didn't). Listening to that tape now reveals Metallica was definitely sloppy in 1982, but they made up for it by being fast and heavy; they simply bullied their way over such details as precision. That would come later.

They played The Waldorf again the following month at another Metal Monday. Word of mouth about the band had spread since the previous show, and a sizeable crowd was on hand at The Waldorf on November 29, 1982, for their first S.F. headlining appearance—a show advertised as "The Maniacs Return." Coincidentally, one of the opening bands was Exodus with Kirk Hammett.

Earlier that week, Lars told me that some guy from Riot's management might be at the show. This inspired me to make a cardboard sign that simply said, "Metallica Fuckin' Rules!" As the show drew to a frenzied conclusion, a friend took the sign, waved it around, and threw it onto the drum riser. Months later, I visited the band at their new home in El Cerrito, and noticed the sign hanging on a bedroom door.

James, The Waldorf, S.F., March 29, 1982.

The band played a new song at the Waldorf called "Whiplash," and they also taped the show, which was released as the "Metal up Your Ass" live tape. For some reason they were unable to tape through the mixing board, so the recording was made with a boom box propped above the mixing board and facing the stage.

Following The Waldorf show, the band was asked to take part in a benefit for Ron Quintana's *Metal Mania*. The show was scheduled for the next night, November 30, at the Mabuhay Gardens on Broadway. (Located across the street from The Stone, the Mab was the center of the S.F. punk scene in the late

Seventies.) They stayed the extra day and played the show. As on the previous night, Exodus (with Kirk) opened. A specific memory I have from this show is of James interrupting the soundcheck to keep a bouncer from throwing me out because I wasn't a member of the band. This was also the band's final performance with original bassist Ron McGovney.

In January 1983 Lars called to say that the band would be in the Bay Area to jam with their new bassist for the first time. The rehearsal took place in El Cerrito at the house, the soon-to-be infamous Metallica mansion. The band had set up their equipment in the family room of the small, two-bedroom house. Lars's drums were up against the couch and James's Marshall stack was against the fireplace. Lars introduced me to Cliff Burton, who was extremely friendly, as he would always be—whenever he saw me at a show or on the street he went out of his way to talk to me.

They jammed for several hours, while I sat on the couch behind Lars, taking pictures. The four or five other "witnesses" present were crammed into hallways and corners. After they finished, I took some posed photos of the band in the family room and in the backyard. These were the first pictures of Metallica with Cliff.

I saw Cliff with his old band Trauma when they opened for Saxon in April, 1982, and I remember how amazing he was, especially when he used a drinking glass as a slide during his solo. While Cliff was still in the band, Trauma recorded a demo for the song "Such a Shame." I saw Trauma again after Cliff joined Metallica; coincidentally, they were opening for the post-Kirk Exodus! Cliff was at the show, and the two of us went to the front of the stage for Trauma's set, where he enthusiastically headbanged to his old band.

Cliff's debut with Metallica was at The Stone on March 5, 1983. Once again, one of the opening bands was Exodus with Kirk. My response to this show appeared in *Metal Mania* #10.

METALLICA
The Stone, San Francisco
March 5th, 1983

Six months have passed since Metallica's San Francisco debut, and in that time the group has built up a large, rabid following in the Bay Area. This particular show was dubbed "The Night of the Banging Head," and was the debut of bassist Cliff Burton. As a crowd of 300 or so filed into The Stone, the scene was set for what turned out to be the heaviest show in recent S.F.H.M. history!

Metallica, those Supreme Metal Gods, those Purveyors of Raging Sonic Decapitation, those Rabid Vodka-Powered Maniacs, blew our faces off as they stormed onstage through a flurry of smoke and blinding lights and got things really banging with "Hit the Lights." It was time to DIE!

As is their style, the band went from power to power as they steamed through "The Mechanix" and "Phantom Lord," leaving the headbanging hordes thrashed and raging—and it was only three songs into the set! The autobiographical "Motorbreath" was as fast as ever, and even more plaster cascaded from the ceiling. The group incorporated some new lighting and effects at this show, and the results were staggering! Their live show is now complete and is the most effective of any club band I've seen!

Next up was the fiery cauldron of "Jump in the Fire," and then that war machine that eats its way across the land, "No Remorse"! DEATH, DEATH, RESOUNDING DEATH! And still, METALLICA mercilessly hacked through their list of nuclear soul shatterers. "Seek and Destroy" found its target and drilled our eardrums, as the headbanging of the crowd, and band, intensified.

The moment many had been waiting for soon arrived: bassist Cliff Burton's solo spot! Cliff built his solo from a haunting classical guitar-sounding ballad up to a crescendo of some of the fastest, most apocalyptic bass raging ever performed! Throughout his symphony, Cliff (a.k.a. God!) utilized his wah-wah pedal to attain sounds that most would believe impossible; you could swear he was playing lead guitar, not bass! As his solo built to its conclusion, drummer-supreme Lars Ulrich and maestro of the six-string Dave Mustaine leaped into an awesome jam that had heads bobbing violently and hair flying in all directions. Then, in one swift action, they were rejoined by vocalist/rhythm guitar/rager James Hetfield and sped into that ear-bleeding anthem "Whiplash." Closing the set were the two Diamond Head classics "Am I Evil" and "The Prince."

For their well-deserved and loudly requested encores, Metallica brought back Blitzkrieg's bombastic "Blitzkrieg" (Raging Metallic Death!) and then obliterated everyone and everything as they sliced into that anthem to end all anthems, the almighty ode to headbangers, "Metal Militia."

With the addition of Cliff Burton, Metallica now has the heaviest and fastest lineup assembled! With dates confirmed in New York in early April and their debut album expected later this year, things are beginning to happen for the band!

Another show at The Stone was booked for a couple of weeks

later, on March 19, and dubbed "The Heaviest Night of Your Life." This gig was videotaped, and the version of "Whiplash" from this night, along with excerpts from a pre-show interview, appear on the *Cliff 'em All* video. It was also the band's final San Francisco appearance with Dave Mustaine, and their last before leaving for New York to record *Kill 'em All*. Both shows drew large crowds and the band performed an instrumental prelude to "Phantom Lord" called "When Hell Freezes Over." This composition later appeared on *Ride the Lightning* as "Call of Ktulu." At these shows, the band sold the original black "Metal up Your Ass" shirts (not the machete-through-the-toilet design).

I saw Exodus a couple of times when Kirk was with them, and several of his riffs from Exodus later turned up in Metallica songs. For example, the bridge in "Creeping Death" is from an old Exodus song titled "Die By His Hand." During the Kirk-era Exodus recorded a three-song demo that contained the songs "Whipping Queen," "Death & Domination," and "Warlords." The band participated in the second *Metal Mania* benefit held on February 20, 1983, and I reviewed the show in *Metal Mania* #10.

EXODUS
The Mabuhay Gardens, San Francisco
February 20, 1983

Exodus are undeniably the fastest maturing band on the S.F.H.M. scene, and at this show they proved this beyond a shadow of a doubt! The band slashed through a 45-minute performance of high-intensity obliteration that had the dandruff flying down in front. The twin-axe attack of Gary Holt and Kirk Hammett provided a titanium spearhead for the steamrolling rhythm section of Jeff Andrews (bass) and Tom Hunting (drums), that in turn provided the backdrop for the elbow-in-the-face vocals of Paul Baloff.

The high point of the show occurred during Exodus' final song, when two inebriated maniacs (whose identities shall remain anonymous) leaped onstage midsong and commenced to thrash and headbang as the band shifted into fifth gear. Not satisfied with just a headbanging duet, these two decibel mongers dragged a close friend of theirs onstage with them, and the three of them (hint: they make up 3/4 of a certain Metal band) proceeded to rage their way about the stage as Exodus dodged out of their way. Following this example, at least half a dozen bangers invaded the stage, and as the song reached its bombastic conclusion, the Mab's stage resembled the set of American BANGstand! At the last moment, roadies and stagehands moved in to clear the area, and luckily no one was seriously injured, save for a few dozen cases of whiplash. (Note: the three drunken and anonymous maniacs were Dave Mustaine, James Hetfield, and Lars Ulrich.)

The release of *Kill 'em All* was a major event for the S.F.H.M. scene. Before its release, I took some friends visiting from Canada over to the Metallica house for an advance listening of the album. The listening party soon degenerated into a drunken air guitar session, led by James, in the living room.

The "Kill 'em All for One" tour with Raven closed with shows on September 1-3, 1983 on the now defunct Keystone club circuit. These shows were Kirk's debut hometown appearances with the band, and his old friends Exodus opened the second show in Berkeley. My review of these shows appeared in *Whiplash* #1.

An early band publicity photo.

KILL 'EM ALL FOR ONE TOUR REVIEW
September 1983

This summer saw the joint Raven/Metallica "Kill 'em All For One" tour winding its way across America, leaving smashed

craniums and snapped necks in its wake. Kicking off in New Brunswick, New Jersey, on July 27, the tour concluded on September 3, in San Francisco. Highlights of the tour included a wild show August 13, in Chicago, where, with video cameras rolling, Kirk Hammett lost his guitar in a tug-of-war with some overzealous fans (the instrument was later recovered by roadies).

On the other side of the coin, the low point was unanimously identified to be the bleak and hostile redneck strongholds of Arkansas and Oklahoma. The bands were booked into halls ranging from 14,000-seat convention centers to huge barns in the middle of pastures, where barely a hundred or so people turned up for the shows. Maybe the two Metal bands should have hooked up with Waylon and Willie. Imagine the jamming version of "On the Road Again" they could've done! Yee-Haw!

At last, though, their arduous journey brought them to California. Following a one night stand at the Country Club in L.A. on August 30, their dirt and dust encrusted U-Hauls with "No Life 'til Frisco" scrawled on the sides, pulled into the Bay Area for the final three dates of the tour. Needless to say, the Bay Area Bangers turned out *en masse* for these, the heaviest shows of the year.

Palo Alto was the sight of the first night's thrash session. In keeping with its poser tradition, the folks at the Keystone Palo Alto refused to let the bands use their P.A. system, which they had been dragging with them all the way from New Jersey, and also told them that the volume level had to be kept down so as not to disturb the neighbors!

Metallica's problems began almost as soon as they hit the stage. During the opener "Hit the Lights," some degenerate moron in the front row used a knife to slash the cord leading from Kirk Hammett's effects board, causing his guitar and amp to fall silent. With the song finished, Kirk threw the axe down in disgust and walked off stage and, at the same moment, half of Lars Ulrich's cymbals inexplicably fell over.

As can be guessed, these mishaps created an awkward delay. James Hetfield and Cliff Burton did their best to amuse the crowd as roadies scampered about trying to piece everything back together. After around 10 minutes of this chaos Metallica was able to continue, and at once stormed through a vicious assault on the senses with "The Four Horsemen," the instrumental "When Hell Freezes Over," which segued into "Phantom Lord," "Seek and Destroy," "Metal Militia," and the set-closing "Whiplash" (with the "Pulling Teeth" bass intro). For reasons unknown, even to the band, "No Remorse" was left out of the set that night, but

Opposite: Lars backstage in Palo Alto, Halloween, 1983.

"Motorbreath" served as the band's encore. Also, as part of the curtain call, Kirk Hammett, who was making his debut Bay Area appearance with Metallica, performed a great solo spot, complete with Ritchie Blackmore-style guitar treatment.

Despite the problems and the typically lackluster South Bay crowd Metallica delivered a deadly set, and it was great to see 'em onstage again after six months! While it definitely wasn't the smoothest Metallica, it was certainly an ominous prelude to the aural destruction of the next two nights! One down, two to go...

The following night in Berkeley, Metallica were heralded as if

they were the second coming of Christ: the noise from the packed Keystone as the houselights went down was phenomenal! The band ripped into "Hit the Lights" engulfed in smoke and light as the club erupted into the most furious headbanging seen here since Metallica's last shows in March. The set was the same as the previous night, except that "No Remorse" made its welcome appearance and "Metal Militia" did encore duties.

An extension had been added to the front of the stage to give the bands more room, but halfway through the show the Bay Bangers had clambered onto it to bang at eye level with the band. In a desperate attempt to clear the stage, the Keystone goons threw many of the crazed punters back into the seething mass that was the dance floor, but their efforts only resulted in more rabid bangers climbing up to take their place!

As the evening intensified and wound down to the show-closer "Whiplash," the band found themselves stranded onstage. The dressing rooms in Berkeley are located in the rear of the club, and the only way to reach them is to exit the stage and walk through the club. Considering the well-meaning, but completely rabid crowd, this route appeared impossible. The band didn't mind engaging their fans, but their road crew was obviously not used to such volatile adulation, and they threw, hit, and shoved the punters out of the way.

After several minutes of riot conditions, Kirk returned to perform his solo spot. The rest of Metallica then joined him for an apocalyptic, death-dealing version of "Metal Militia," complete

with the traditional "Metal up Your Ass" crowd participation part. With Metallica's set completed, the bar was mobbed by the thoroughly thrashed and thirsty bangers in need of liquid relief. Two down, one to go...

James at S.F.'s Record Vault for an autograph signing session, 1983.

The next afternoon found the bands at The Record Vault in San Francisco for a good, old-fashioned autograph session. A great time was had by all, as Mercyful Fate wailed from the stereo and the bands kept themselves amused by browsing for records, signing autographs and smashing the occasional *Men at Work* album. This lasted a couple of hours, and then it was off to The Stone for the soundcheck.

As this evening's show was to be the final date of the tour, the bands pulled out all the stops in order to make it memorable. The Stone has been the site of several Metallica shows (their "home turf," you might call it) and *deja vu* reigned supreme: it was Berkeley all over again! The SRO crowd went apeshit in response to the "San Francisco, will you welcome home, METALLICAAAAA!!!!!" introduction to "Metal Militia."

During Raven's set, Lars and James high-kicked their way across the stage, spraying beer at Raven as they danced by. They were followed by Cliff, who literally flooded the stage by dousing everyone and everything with water. It was amazing no one was electrocuted. Later, to close out the show and the tour, James and Lars returned to join Raven for backup vocals and some rampaging air guitar. Even though the guitars wielded by the Metallica boys weren't plugged in, there no doubt now exist bangers who now consider Lars Ulrich a Guitar God! Yes, all those years of tennis-racket wielding certainly paid off! As soon as the "all star jam" was completed, James took a flying leap into the audience.

✠

On Halloween, 1983, the band blitzed the Keystone in Palo Alto, and on November 25 & 26, they did shows at the Keystone Berkeley, and The Stone in S.F. (both dates had Armored Saint opening). They played three new songs at these performances: "Fight Fire with Fire," "Ride the Lightning," and "Creeping Death." (A demo of these songs, plus "Call of Ktulu," was recorded around this time.) The San Francisco show featured a hilarious "Fuck You James" chant to bring the band back for encores. These were Metallica's final Bay Area appearances for eight months.

Their next Bay Area gig was a surprise show advertised under the pseudonym "Kill 'em All," at the tiny Mabuhay Gardens on July 20, 1984. Metallica had just returned from their first European tour, and this show was a sloppy affair reminiscent of their first S.F. gigs. The show, which the band opened with "Blitzkrieg," was stopped three times as fans invaded the stage.

The release of *Ride the Lightning* blew the floodgates of popularity wide open for Metallica; their days as a local club band were over. On their subsequent tour, they returned one last time to the Keystone Palo Alto on March 13, 1985. This was the band's final "official" club appearance in the Bay Area ever. They also played two San Francisco shows on the 14th and 15th at the 1,500-seat Kabuki Theater. One of my favorite Metallica memories is of something that occurred at the first Kabuki show: I arrived late, and the band was already a couple of songs into their set. I fought my way towards the stage and ended up in front of Cliff, who was in his standard osntage stance: one foot on the monitor and his hair flying everywhere as he headbanged. For a moment, he looked out over the crowd. Out of the hundreds of anonymous faces in front of him, he recognized mine. A smile came to his face and he shouted my name several times. That moment made being late to the show unimportant.

On October 12, 1991, nearly 10 years since their first San Francisco show, Metallica played the Bay Area again, this time to kick off the American leg of their 1991/92 Tour. The show began just like the old days, with the band's traditional intro tape: "Lust for Gold" from *The Good, The Bad, & The Ugly* soundtrack. However, unlike a decade earlier, this show was at Oakland Stadium, not The Stone—and there were about 50,000 fans.

Things have changed.

San Francisco Heavy Metal
The Birth of a Scene
by Ron Quintana

IN 1979 I turned 18, attended a year of college, and moved out, for the first time!, into a hard-rockin' household of like-minded metal fans that called themselves the "Anti-Disco Movement" (A.D.M.) of San Francisco. I devoted myself to music, often buying 10 albums a day at the expense of all other things, sometimes

James during the band's first jam with Cliff, El Cerrito, January 1983.

including food. Soon I had every record and 8-track of all the heavy bands I'd heard about.

There were no local metal bands playing around, aside from the old Yesterday and Today, and the ubiquitous high school bands. We only knew about bands from San Francisco and the few East Bay bands we learned of through contacts at "Day on the Green" or Y&T concerts in Oakland or Keystone Berkeley gigs. This is how we met Paul Baloff and his friend Denny Gill's Diamond group, who we'd seen at parties. The East Bay scene didn't really make any noise for several years, and the West Bay scene was still in its infancy or dominated by the thriving New Wave. In our search for the great crunching chord, we would check out punk or jazz fusion shows just to hear a few good riffs or interesting musicianship. The energy of the punk scene was especially fun, but not quite what we desired; it just didn't hit the right nerves.

In the newer British music papers, especially *Sounds,* that occasionally I was able to unearth, I read about all these bands with strange names that I'd seen reviewed and listed in heavy metal mail-order catalogs.

Once in a while our Tower Import or used record shops would get some of these new groups, but it was never enough. Being such rabid fans, we collected any odd albums or singles, buttons, patches, and photos we could find, starting with groups like Motorhead, Maiden, and Leppard. Our import tastes grew through information from UK fanzines; radio was and always has been nonexistent, in terms of heavy metal.

In 1980 KSAN, the underground giant that revolutionized FM radio in the Sixties, before going country, began playing its rare library of archival concert tapes. I recorded most of them and traded with friends to get more rare stuff but couldn't get enough. I'd seen little ads in *Circus* or *Sounds* advertising concert tapes for sale, and I started sending for their lists and buying tapes of my favorite bands. Soon I made up my own list and started trading because it was a cheaper and often faster way to collect music.

I searched out more collector's magazines, the best of which was *Audio Trader*, born in Berkeley in late 1980. Editor Stuart Sweetow was totally into the audio and video collecting scene, and he later encouraged me to write about the rise of the new metal bands for his magazine. I started writing about the New Wave of British Heavy Metal, obscure metal groups and other stuff I had traded ferociously. By 1981, my list and contacts had grown overseas. I received the first *Aardschok* magazine from Holland, and traded with its editors and readers. The first real underground all-metal 'zine, it showed me that I could do something similar, too. My friends and I had often talked about having a metal-lovers club or opening our own record store, or starting a metal magazine, but such ventures seemed too expensive or involved to be feasible.

✠

Around this time, metal-loving friends and I frequented a party hangout known as "Strawberry Hill," located at the top of a rise on the island in the middle of Stow Lake, in the center of Golden Gate Park. It was about as rural, open, and far away from neighbors and cops that you could get in San Francisco. We climbed up there to get drunk and very loud every Friday and Saturday night. There usually were 20 or 30 kids running around with 6-packs and boom-boxes, having stereo-blasting battles, and people who would drift to which one had the best metal.

One night, I was partying on "The Hill" with other bangers Sherwood Brewer, Ian Kallen, and Paul Baloff, when over walked

Rich Burch (a.k.a. "Skitchy") and some overly patched jeans-jacket guy who talked funny and introduced himself as Lars. He had more British patches than any of us had ever seen, and he talked about bands that we'd only read about on occasion, if we'd even heard of them. He had tapes of some of them, and Lars and I immediately discovered our common interest in Diamond Head, the heaviest new group, and the fact that I had live tapes of them that he didn't have.

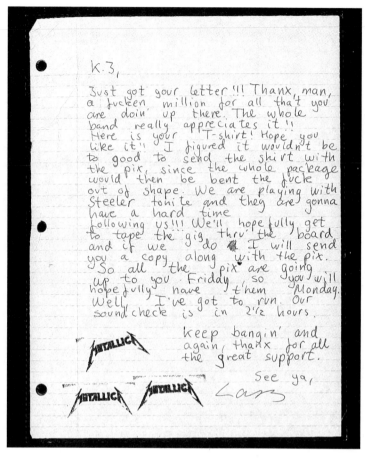

Lars was part of the tape-trading underground, and the buddy of an Alice Cooper and Iron Maiden fanatic named Brian Slagel—who had an even bigger tape list than mine! So later that night, Lars, Skitchy, and I hung out and talked about nothing but new metal and rode around in Lars's green Pacer, listening to his tapes of Parallex, Savage, and a whole slew of new English groups.

Lars would visit S.F. and crash on my floor. He broke my cassette deck by constantly playing and rewinding my best live Diamond Head tapes (no doubt trying to figure out the lyrics to "Am I Evil," or "Helpless," or "The Prince"), but always brought up enough cool tapes and 'zines to make me forget about any problems. He talked about seeing Deep Purple and idolizing Ian Paice, and was excited about getting his drum kit over from Denmark so he could practice.

We'd heard about a cool new all-metal store in Walnut Creek, so we hopped on BART one day and found The Record Exchange. It was Heavy Nirvana for us, with tons of import albums, singles, and 'zines (although Lars already had most of them), and the store soon became the metal center of the Bay Area. I found the first issue of *Kerrang!* magazine there, and was inspired to write and tell them of my plight. I wanted desperately to put out a metal fanzine, so in my letter I solicited writers to join me.

✠

The Church of Metal was a thrash house in the industrial section of S.O.M.A. in San Francisco. One resident was the Seattle emigre Kurt Vanderhoof, who lived there after quitting the punk band The Lewd. He decided to start up a heavier, more Motorhead-type group with some guys from the S.F. progressive metal rockers Leviathan, who saw him at a punk show wearing a Rush shirt and introduced themselves. Leviathan guitarist Rick Condron also lived at the Church of Metal, and he and the others jammed constantly and dubbed themselves Metal Church in the fall of 1980. By December, they'd loaned me a three-song rehearsal tape (with the songs "Red Skies," "Mercilous Onslaught," and "Heads Will Roll") and told me not to give it to anyone. So naturally, I sent it to everyone, and the Metal Church legend was born. Although

they never played a gig, they had an enormous reputation in the tape-trading world. Even that renowned tape-trading jet-setter/ tennis prodigy/metal fan Lars Ulrich heard them while he was in the Bay Area in the summer of 1981.

Spastic Children: L to R - James McDaniel, Cliff, Fred Cotton, James, 1985.

However, I didn't see much of Lars for the next year or so. He was scheduled to show up downtown later in June to audition for a vacant drummer slot with Metal Church. Kurdt and Rick complained that he never showed up or even called, and when he disappeared we all wrote him off as a big-talking flake. No one could reach him in L.A., so we all forgot about the Dane.

Only Skitchy could contact Lars, and when Motorhead came to America in early July, both followed the band around California. They even hung out on Motorhead's tour bus and got to be good buddies with the band. Skitchy followed the Motorhead brigade (on tour with Ozzy), but Lars stayed in L.A. preparing for a trip back home to Copenhagen and didn't talk to Burch until 1982.

✠

In the meantime, although they weren't my favorite band, Motorhead was the ugliest, fastest, noisiest, and most uncommercial group around. Their sound was a strong indicator of the future of metal. After their concert, I was inspired to review it for *Audio Trader*, but as I had all these photos and other bands to write about, I just started informally laying out my updated audio tape list with a few pages of articles and pictures. By August, I had way more local news, photos, and stories than there was a tape list! So I just dropped my list, stapled and folded 8 1/2" X 11" pages in the middle and turned it sideways into a 24-page mini-magazine (or "fanzine") entitled *Metal Mania*!

Simultaneously, in September, Brian Slagel sent me the first issue of his magazine, *The New Heavy Metal Revue,* and I traded him mine. *N.H.M.R.* was always better organized and backed and looked more like a real magazine than *Metal Mania*, making me jealous. But we had a friendly L.A./S.F. rivalry anyway.

Kerrang! #4 printed (almost) my entire letter, which asked other metal fans from across the world to correspond with me, trade music, and collaborate on a fanzine. Eventually, I received over a hundred letters! Most were silly and useless from strange Britons, but many were from fed up and well-motivated American bangers (Harold Oimoen, Brian Lew, K.J. Doughton, Lantz Shapiro, Bob Nalbandian, and Patrick Scott), as well as other fanzine/ magazine editors and writers who wanted to (and eventually did) write for *Metal Mania* (Bernard Doe, Derek Oliver, Steve Hammonds, and Geoff Banks, from the U.K.).

✠

Lars had "disappeared" in August to England, where he met his idols Diamond Head. Meanwhile, *Metal Mania* was going great, and as soon as Metallica played its first gigs, our L.A. correspondents, Bob Nalbandian and Patrick Scott, wrote an L.A. Heavy Metal review featuring the 'tallicats. In what emerged as the first-ever article written on Metallica, Scott mentioned that the band "had the potential to become U.S. Metal Gods."

In March, *Metal Mania* hit the weekly radio airwaves! Co-editor Ian Kallen had done some Heavy Metal special shows for KUSF FM God Howie Klein that had gotten a good response. The two asked me to join them, and we were soon given a regular late Saturday night time slot (Sunday morning, actually—from 1-3:00 a.m.), and "Rampage Radio" was born. We started out playing all the heaviest old and new import records and local demos. Gradually, more and more local bands formed and sent us demos. My concerts and non-local demos formed the rest of the shows, along

with the odd band coming down for an interview. It gradually snowballed into the 2-8:00 a.m. shift, where it remains.

Metallica with Ron Quintana's Metal Mania fanzine, 1983.

Along with the growing success of both *Metal Mania* and "Rampage Radio," a new Heavy Metal record store opened in San Francisco, the infamous Record Vault, which soon became the predominant center of metal retailing in the Bay Area. With more local bands popping up, The Old Waldorf started booking "Metal Mondays," starting with the infamous Motley Crue/Anvil Chorus gig in April, and other clubs booked similar shows/nights.

Trauma headlined one such night on May 3, and I was rather impressed—not so much by the bassist's amazing playing and soloing as by the twin Flying "V" lead guitarists' choreographed

moves and matching leather pants! The lead singer, decked out in similar duds, looked and sounded like Rob Halford, and one guitarist bore a striking resemblance to Buck Dharma. They were a striking lot, but their music, while heavy, was pedestrian.

✠

By July 1982, I'd devoted myself to *Metal Mania* and earned enough dough to take off to Europe for six months of travel, schmoozing and depravity. While I was gone, Metallica's legend grew, and through my friends in Europe I'd see articles in *Northwest Metal* and *Aardschok* about the band. In England, I visited the famed Marquee club and Reading Festival and saw most of the New Wave of British Heavy Metal bands I'd only heard about before. The best were Diamond Head, Budgie, Tank, Tygers of Pan Tang, Raven, and great foreign bands like Bow Wow, Baron Rojo,

and Anvil. I traveled all over the continent and almost forgot about music. I did manage to see Accept, Electric Sun, and a few other European bands, but none were were as impressive as Mercyful Fate. They'd just signed to *Aardschok's* Rave-On Records. Mercyful Fate became my favorite band for the next several years until they broke up in 1985. They were great musicians with incredibly complex songs, and so fucking heavy!

James modeling his homemade Spastic Children T-shirt November 1986.

✠

Back to America in December 1982, weary and worn-out, I returned to a thriving Bay Area metal scene, which, according to reports, had been conquered and dominated by this L.A. band of Lars's named Metallica. I'd been impressed by their demo and live tapes, and just missed seeing the *Metal Mania* benefit they'd played at the Mabuhay Gardens. I was intrigued by everything I

heard and called Lars, who said they were moving to the Bay Area.

✠

Aside from the buzz on Metallica, I heard a lot about Exodus. Little did I know that not only was it my old buddy Paul Baloff's band, but that he was the singer (maybe sing is not the right word!). Having just finished *Metal Mania* #9 and at work on #10, I asked Paul if Exodus could play a benefit for the magazine with Anvil Chorus, Blind Illusion, and Warning. The L.A. guys from Metallica were there, and they even hopped onstage for Exodus' encore. Everyone hung out and partied after the gig, which was one of Exodus' last with Kirk.

At this time, I was hanging out at the Carlson house a lot. Skitchy was always around since he lived less than a mile north of there. We drank a lot of vodka. I particularly remember going with the gang to one party at photographer Jenny Raisler's house. The

James at Roskilde displaying a Metal Mania.

typically inebriated Metalli-guitarists happened to get on opposite sides of the bathroom door at the same time, with Dave trying to get out and James trying to get in. Naturally the door window broke, and there was much yelling until Dave spat beer all over Raisler's personal Y&T wall photos (and calling the local band "wankers"). The Alcoholicas were tossed out on their ears.

Throughout 1982, I had a lot of contact with a guy from New Jersey named John Zazula, who had an underground retail store named "Rock 'n Roll Heaven." He often sold my 'zine through distributors. He set up some cool-sounding shows around Halloween with Riot, Anvil, The Rods, and others. By Christmas, he was impressed by the great response to the Metallica demos brought in by store regulars. He called me a few times in a frantic state, trying to "find this Metallica gang" he'd read about in my 'zine, and I tried to get him in touch with them. Eventually, he talked them into going back East to record for him, and launched his new record label "Megaforce." It sounded kind of shady at first, but Johnny was a hell of a fast talker, and he convinced everyone what a great idea it was.

In March the Metallipace picked up, and the band planned to

Kirk and pal Larry Lalonde of Primus at The Stone, 1985.

head east after playing a couple of Stone shows "for the Bay Area Bangers" Back then, shows were a little different than they are today. The old U.S. metal salute—the raised pounding fist—was slowly being replaced by the European "headbang." Americans usually just stood there and shook their fist or "prong" (index and pinky fingers raised), Europeans usually shook their heads very fast and violently to the beat. It's amusing to see an entire audience, bodies frozen, flail madly to the music with their heads and hair! At most Dutch and British concerts I attended, the headbangers barely even looked at the band, except between songs! As soon as a note was hit they just stood in place with their heads bopping up and down, their eyes often closed and mouths twisted into expressions of ecstasy and pain. Some would often play an imaginary instrument ("air guitar") along to the music. There was none of the punk thrashing, headwalking, and stage-diving that was to sweep the metal crossover scene years later.

Metallica audiences reflected a sense of style that was a mixture of U.S. and British. Dress usually consisted of lots of denim and some leather. Jean pants and jackets were *de rigueur* and vests covered in all the latest pins, patches, and buttons were to be envied. For some reason, studded leather was big. Leather bracelets, arm bands, hats, and more stuff covered in square silver studs were way popular. Like Rhinestones to Liberace, some kids (often "posers") covered themselves in these ornaments to a degree that would make even Rob Halford wince!

That brings up the point of poseurs and wankers. A "wanker" referred to just about any asshole, while a "poseur" was anyone who followed all the latest trends, but was always one step behind the crowd—a wannabe. Eventually, however, a "poser" came to be anyone who didn't like your kind of music (i.e. heavy). If they were really heavy, the hardcore bangers like Mustaine or Baloff would talk about "killing posers" and other such silly stuff. The Bay Area metal scene ran the gamut from the pop Van Halen or Motley Crue clones to all-out Motorhead maniacs who often dabbled in the hardcore punk scene. The scene was still so small that devotees of all the genres would go to the clubs to see shows. So all these little groups would be spread out in some hall, righteously bickering among themselves over what was the best kind of music. It was fun!

The March Metallica concerts were no different, but the future was unfolding as the music and the crowds polarized. There were some great, monumental gigs, such as Cliff's first with the band and Dave's last in S.F. We all anxiously awaited the former, but really had no warning about the latter. Dave was a maniac, but that was quite a bit of Metallica's appeal.

March was filled with parties and get-togethers at the Carlson pad. On March 16, they recorded their raging third demo of "Whiplash" and "No Remorse" which they gave out the next week. As usual, it was dominated by various vodkas (before anyone could even pronounce "Stolichnaya"), and obligatory headbanging and air guitar jams. As usual, Dave drank earlier, more and faster than anyone else present and passed out by nine—before the party had even started! This was ignored, as everyone just partied around and over Dave, occasionally trying to wake him up, drag him around, or pose for photos with his lifeless frame.

That party was particularly obnoxious, as most of the people who showed up were East Bayers led by the demented Exodus gang, most notably Paul Baloff and Gary Holt. Those guys were evil and real crazy back then. At one point in the evening, I found myself helping them to thrash some car! At a party the week earlier, it had been broken down and left in the driveway. Whittaker was pissed off at the guy and wanted it out, and so didn't mind our demolishing it. We ran wild, tweaking the doors, smashing the dash, and tearing up the interior's foam padding (subsequently added to the garage noise barriers!). The next day, Lars and James posed for photos on top of the car's dented roof, and loaded up their U-Haul van to head out on their infamous first trip to New Jersey. But the automobile story did not end there; the owner returned a few days later, saw his wreck, freaked out, and broke in to steal Lars's stereo in return. It took an extensive apology and cash upon Lars's return to get his beloved box back. I still feel guilty about that one!

We only expected the best for the band on that trip to the East Coast. Little did we suspect that Dave would be fired and replaced by Kirk Hammett.

HULE FLYING 'V' ON THE PIC, EH?
PARIS ET SES MERVEILLES...
5077 - La tour Eiffel (1887-1889), vue la nuit.

HEY FUCK,

WELL IT'S LIKE THE METALLIDIX ALMOST MADE IT TO EUROPE, EH!?! (ABOUT TIME!). SPENT A WEEK IN LONDON AND ARE NOW 'EN ROUTE' TO ZURICH, SWITZERLAND FOR THE FIRST GIG/LIG! SPENT THE LAST FEW REHEARSING AT A GREAT STUDIO. MOTORHEAD WERE AUDITIONING NEW AXMEN IN THE ADJOINING ROOM. SOUNDING AWFULL! LEMMY SAYS 'HI'! (NOT REALLY!!). LARZ LOST IN FRANCE!

PAR AVION

RONALD Q
4340 20th ST.
SAN FRANCISCO.
CA. 94114.
USA.

Metalli-correspondence from Lars to Ron Quintana.

Things worked out very well with Kirk, and *Kill 'em All* came out in August. Not surprisingly, it killed everyone who heard it. I was very pleased to be thanked twice on it: once for myself and a "no thank you" to "Spon Q." (my nickname)–"6 bucks a shot!" The phrase refers to the band's slight disenchantment over the fact that I was trading and selling large numbers of dubs of their demos and live tapes, due to high demand. It was something I did for every band I liked and Metallica was no different. Their subsequent views on bootlegging have mellowed; they are not threatened by it, and are staunch supporters of the fans' need for any material on a preferred band. Mild bootlegging does not detract from a band's revenues. In fact, if anything, it enhances it by helping the band's popularity snowball faster than if there is not enough merchandise available.

The guys returned with Raven on the "Kill 'em All For One" tour to a heroes welcome at the Keystones. I'd met the Raven trio in Europe the year before, and they were great guys. Brothers John and Rob Gallagher and drummer Wacko also had an excellent sense of humor and could be quite entertaining: attributes needed by a new band on its first tour, and I'm sure it helped put Metallica at ease. The tour may not have been a piece of cake, but they were all relaxed when they returned to San Francisco.

The guys hung around town for quite awhile and often dropped by KUSF. They played the Keystones in October and November, then went into hybernation in Copenhagen in early 1984, writing and recording *Ride the Lightning* (they did, however, return in the summer of 1984 to play as "Kill 'em All").

Dave Mustaine, meanwhile, was still in shock, and didn't return to the Bay Area. He wrote long, run-on letters to me and to others, filled with recriminations and vows to start a new band to "kick Metallica's ass." All his stuff was still in the Carlson house, and he eventually had the band send it to him. He was furious with Metallica, but he nevertheless called Lars and the gang to tell them about his new death group, Megadeth, and his plan to still play the original "Mechanix."

When *Ride the Lightning* came out, it quickly alienated many of the hardcore *Kill 'em All* maniacs. Many of the old guard called it a "sell-out/wimp-out," and turned to the faster, newer bands like Slayer, Hellhammer, and Possessed. But far more ate up what was the most accessible Metallica album to date. Meanwhile, Exodus's *Bonded by Blood* debut finally arrived (although tapes of it had been circulated for almost a year.) Many now hailed Exodus as the main Gods of local American metal. Had they quickly followed up their debut, they might possibly have merited that exalted title, but they lost their momentum and began what has been a history of misadventure. Metallica, however, quickly followed up *Ride...* with an even better LP, and secured a limitless future.

✠

1985 was the year of the big metal/punk "crossover." Hard rock bands became faster, punkier and more hardcore, while hardcore bands got heavier. Some bands simply started out somewhere in between. S.O.D. was conceived as the ultimate crossover band, with members of Anthrax and their big hardcore roadie Billy Milano on vocals. They were quite good, combining the metal crunch with punk singing and to-the-point songs.

On November 9, 1985, Paul Baloff, Gary Holt, and some friends sought to create something along the lines of S.O.D at Ruthie's Inn. What they got was noisy and punky, but Gary soloed too much, and the experiment degenerated into a drunken brawl/jam. The band included Heathen's Doug Piercy and Fred Cotton.

James at Ruthies Inn, drumming for Spastic Children, 1985.

Cotton was the Bay Area's answer to Billy Milano and The Mentors' El Duce! A very good friend of James Hetfield and Cliff Burton's, he wanted to start a group. Since he didn't want to go the Duce route, singing and playing drums, he sang while James took over the sticks and Cliff played bass, James "Flunky" McDaniel, their buddy from Pillage Sunday, played guitar. This was Spastic Children, which first assaulted mass ears on January 31, 1986 at Ruthie's. They made pure, inebriated noise to go with silly, Mentors-like lyrics. Hilarious tunes like "Pus Is Great," "I Like Farts," and "Cunt" were rather self-explanatory and amusing.

Metallica's attainment of near-deity status allowed James and Cliff to have some fun as well as the chance to prove they were human. So they got as un-sober as possible before a gig and went onstage and goofed off. Most people did not get the joke, and stood there chanting their desire to hear "Creeping Death" or some other god song—and the Children would just burp and fart and spit at the audience. It was all very amusing.

Spastik played at the Rock on Broadway on February 20, and again on March 8, with The Mentors. Metallica had to tour for *Master of Puppets* with Ozzy, so the Children went into hiding, except for an unexpected gig June 21, back at Ruthie's. Apparently, Lars had broken his left foot, Ozzy was hit in the head with a bottle, and bad publicity plagued the tour: combined, these factors prompted the Metalli-break. Their next real visit home was in August, after James broke his left arm skateboarding. As James couldn't drum, he joined Fred as a frontman on August 29, at the

Above: Cliff at Ruthies Inn during unannounced gig, 1985.

next Spastik show at the Rock on Broadway. Jumbo, the big lead singer of Pillage Sunday filled in on drums while the corn-rowed James and Fred danced around and taunted the small audience, who were mostly on hand to see a German punk band.

✠

Metallica soon left for Europe and the ill-fated September tour. We soon got word of a terrible accident. Cliff was dead. No warning, no signs. Just like that, he was gone. I'd known people who'd died before, but Cliff's death caused me to reflect quite a bit on life. Many people had never experienced death and were actually quite shattered, whether they knew Cliff or not. There was quite a bit of shock and mourning. On October 7, I went to Cliff's funeral in Castro Valley.

In November Metallica went back on tour and returned around Christmas. By that time, Spastic Children had received a lot of press, and their next gig on January 2, 1987, filled the large Rock on Broadway. For the first time, Spastik felt real pressure to do Metallica songs; there was no denying that. Kirk took over bass playing duties for the sorely-missed Cliff, and the band got drunker and rowdier than ever for the show, which pissed off more people than ever!

Fred and James would often drop by "Rampage Radio" and do their Spastik talk and guest D.J. A couple of times, El Duce would be there and they'd have an obnoxious-a-thon! Sherwood Brewer would join in and thrash them all.

I set up the next Spastik Children show for my Halloween 1987 bash, which was held in a warehouse called "Secret Studios" in the industrial section of S.F. It was a perfect night for Metallica, who dressed up, as did the rest of the attendees. James sported a Danzig-style getup, complete with pale face and a greased-down horn of hair down the center of his face, while Kirk was Dracula, and Flunky and Fred were pirates. They were scheduled in between the Ramones and The Dead Jacksons on a very theatrical night, and didn't get to play until after 2:00 a.m.!

In 1988, the Spastik show was moved to The Stone, and then to The Omni for the next two years. These shows also featured Jim Martin of Faith No More, Jason Newsted on noisy basses, and occasional other guests. They were always packed, but audiences still didn't get it—they still cried out to hear Metallica classics.

As time went on, Metallica achieved huge international fame and their Bay Area visibility dwindled. On October 12, 1991, they headlined "Day on the Green" in Oakland. It was a bit like a headbanger reunion backstage, where many of the old guard fans congregated and became reacquainted with one another. Meanwhile, Metallica blazed through a set that filled me with flashbacks from the previous years—the special era they, more than anyone else, represented. The decade had seen the golden age of Bay Area heavy metal, and Metallica had immortalized that age.

Kirk and friend Mike Meals at Bay Area Halloween bash, 1987.

THE INTERVIEW: JAMES HETFIELD

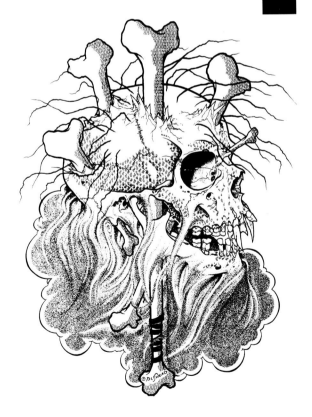

JAMES HETFIELD IS a lanky, hulking lumberjack of a man with a lived-in look showing the abrasion and decay, both physical and psychic, that he's unapologetically undergone in the past decade. Eleven years ago, in a Brea High School yearbook photo, he sported a Donny Osmond grin which complemented his accompanying post-graduation resolution to "make music and get rich." He looked innocent and full of pizazz, but, after a decade of achieving his dreams, he reflects doom, gloom, and menace.

Meeting James at his condo-styled home in Novato, California, however, he's an entirely more placid character. Enjoying a rare domestic evening before flying to Seattle to finish off the colossal Metallica/Guns N' Roses stadium tour, James seems ready for a break. He has no butler or limo and greets me at the door and gives me a tour of his home.

Although complemented by a billiard room, a sizeable kitchen complete with a cast-iron stove, a 'round-the-house wooden deck that looks out over the surrounding hills which he owns, and a sportsman's den adorned with mounted ducks, wolf heads, and animal skins, such features are the loudest highlights of what is actually a sparse, airy escape; in fact, not a gold record is to be found anywhere. Even Metallica members need a break from Metallica.

Opposite: James on the "Damaged Justice" tour, 1989.

In 10 years of falling over his band, like a noise-craving parasite, I'd never had the opportunity to interview the enigmatic co-founder. The first thing that struck me was his complete lack of pretension; he calls it like he sees it.

While such brutal frankness might startle some, it's this quality which embodies the spirit of Metallica. James is the guy who gives the world the finger and gets away with it. By the time the record's over or the concert has ended, the score has been evened out. While drilling James on the band's history, I was not surprised to find that after all these years of stalking stages and downing beers, a few details had trickled out of his well-worn cranium. On the other hand, his recollection of other obscure tidbits and unlikely anecdotes made it clear that the human touches and friendships in his life carry more importance. Unlike his comrade Lars Ulrich, who is a social missile seeking out constant, unending activity, Hetfield likes his quiet time; there's no pressure to hold up a conversation because he probably prefers silence to surface talk; however, when the tape rolls, the words flow freely as he reflects on Metallica's greatest moments.

You played festivals like Castle Donnington's "Monsters of Rock" show, which is infamous for the number of things hurled onstage. How do you deal with such crazy behavior?

We've had plenty of stuff come on the stage. In either Vancouver of Portland, I got hit in the head with a bottle. It kinda made me woozy for a while, and I didn't know if I should stop or not. I had blood comin' down my head, but I wasn't fallin' over. Since then, when bottles come up, or things that can hurt us, we'll stop the fuckin' show.

There's been a couple of shows where I've seen darts on the stage. It's like, people are throwin' darts up there—that's no good! Dipped in what, who fuckin' knows? At one of the Donnington shows, we had pieces of pig flyin' up. Someone had slaughtered a pig and threw it up there. You get all kinds of piss thrown up. Basically 'cause fans are there waitin' for the show, drinkin' these liters of cider, or whatever, and they don't want to lose their place in line, so they piss in their bottle and chuck it. I remember one kid trying to sneak in a chainsaw to a gig, under his trenchcoat. Who fuckin' knows why? Maybe he was gonna get his way up to the front REAL quick! WRAAAARRRRRR! Ha, ha, ha!

But there's mostly demo tapes, flowers, flyers, underwear, bras, and other crap that fly up there. You find bras that would fuckin' fit a cow. It's like, "God damn! I wouldn't want to see what fit into that thing!" (Laughter.)

On the European leg of the tour supporting Master of Puppets, *Cliff Burton was killed in a bus accident, do you remember what happened?*

One thing that comes to mind was when our tour manager, Bobbie Schneider, was saying, "Okay. Let's get the band together and take them back to the hotel." I'm thinking, "The band? No way! There ain't no band. The band is not 'the band' right now. It's just three guys."

After Cliff's death, Jason joined as the new bassist. Do you remember the auditions?

It was very difficult for us to start auditioning people. Cliff's gear was sitting there in this room and people would be pluggin' into it and trying to play through it. We had no idea who we'd get. We were still pretty much in shock. But we knew we had to get back into it right away. We had this list of people that we kinda had high hopes for. And we saved the best ones for last, I remember. Jason was one of the last guys to audition. There were various people from the Bay Area, and some from L.A. that drove up. We auditioned Les Claypool [bassist for Primus], 'cause he was a pretty good friend of Kirk's. It was fun to play with him, but he was very...funky. We're not really a huge bass-oriented band. Troy Gregory, who went on to play in Flotsam and Jetsam and Prong, was in there somewhere. So was Willie Lange of Laaz Rockit. Those were the three guys left.

I know the guy that ended up in Prong [Gregory] just talked too fuckin' much. He was a little too excited about things (laughter). He wouldn't shut the fuck up, basically. And Willie was real aggressive, but I don't think he could write material, and was a little bit sloppy. Jason had everything we were lookin' for. He was real aggressive, he could play fast, he could play slow, mellow stuff, plus he had written material in Flotsam and was kind of a leader of that band. He basically passed all the tests, including the 'go out drinking with Metallica' test (laughter).

Jason Newsted

There were definitely some people that came in to audition who were basically disrespecting us and Cliff, by just showing up to say, "Ooh, I jammed with Metallica." We did have four songs that everyone was supposed to come in and play. We had one fuckin' guy come in who looked like he was on fuckin' heroin, or some shit. He was playing "Master of Puppets" in the wrong key. We just stopped and said, "Get the fuck outta here!" (Laughter.) We had little cues to tell the roadie guys to stop recording and get them the fuck outta there.

So you were recording the jam sessions with the different bassists?

Yes. We did it in a little studio in Heyward, a little four-track setup. At one point a couple of our roadies found a guy outside taping his buddy in there jamming with us. He had a cassette recorder. The recorder didn't really survive that, and basically got smashed (laughter). Luckily, the bass player got out in one piece. We were ready to fuckin' kill him.

Do fans go over the line between acceptable adulation and being downright irritating?

People do step over the line a lot. We're more of a band that people take personally, you know. It's kinda like, 'They're my band.' They think they know you really well. So they take more advantage of that than I'm sure other fans do with other bands. They'll come and grab you, they'll try to get you to do this or that with 'em. I don't like getting touched by strange people (laughter).

James with Faith No More guitarist, Jim Martin, 1989.

There was a recent thing down in Mexico, where I was sittin' down havin' a nice old talk with my girl down there, and this guy came up and offered to buy me a beer. I said, "Yeah, fine." So he bought a beer, and then he asked if he could sit down. I said, "No. I'm havin' a nice bit of quiet time here." He got offended, I guess, and kinda sat down behind me. I mean, the fuckin' guy asked me if he could sit down, and I'd said no! Eventually, he came over and took his beer away, which was fine by me. Then he kinda started babbling behind my back, calling me "asshole," stuff like that.

I didn't think I needed to put up with that shit, so I invited him over to the table and said, "What's your problem here? Were you complaining to your fuckin' boyfriend over there, or what? If you've got a problem, talk to me. Don't fuckin' whisper shit behind my back! You asked to sit down, and I said no, because I'm busy here!" He said, 'Yeah, man, but I was at your first concert,' and this and that. He was from Berkeley, and basically figured that I owed him something, 'cause he'd been into the band since day one. I thought some other way, and I fuckin' clocked the guy.

A fistfight started, and I ended up getting a bottle over my head by his friend. It got pretty bad. I had blood gushin' from my head and shit, and basically had to hop into the jeep and escape before the Mexican policio arrived. I wasn't keen on spending time in a Mexican jail. If you ever get out, you'll definitely be broke. Basically, the guy thought I'd owed him somethin' for being a fan. It's like, hey, you appreciate our music, you buy our CD's. I like that! It stops there!

You were on the bill for Van Halen's "Monsters of Rock" stadium tour, along with Scorpions, Dokken, and Kingdom Come...

That was hard to remember because we were all really fuckin' drunk during the whole tour. Being on a summer tour, in the United States, with a band like Van Halen, plus us being kinda down on the bill...it was the greatest. You'd go on and play for an hour, and get drunk the rest of the time, walkin' around and harassing women.

Did Metallica get along well with Van Halen?

Oh, yeah. They were partiers, no doubt. I couldn't believe how a band could be around that long and party hardcore like that! We were also on the tour with Dokken; George and Don would be fighting all the fuckin' time. George was a strange character. He'd get drunk and throw his guitar at his roadie, fire him every day. I couldn't understand how he could treat someone like that.

After that tour, I went back to a lot of cities, when we came back out on our own, and people...uh, kinda didn't like me, and I didn't know why. People would come up, "Yeah, you don't remember grabbin' my girlfriend's tits?" or something really rude I'd done when I was really fucked up and didn't basically remember what was going on! You'd come back into town, "Hey, how's it goin'?" and people would give you the evil eye.

Didn't you begin traveling in a private plane instead of a bus?

Yeah. People might think I'm crazy, but I really miss touring on the bus. From the bus we went to a little eight-seater. We'd go into either a little private airport, or a private section of the main airport. That gave us the freedom to spend more time on our own, or get some sleep. Sleeping on the bus for us was not easy after the accident. We couldn't really relax. With every little bump, we'd wake up and freak out. So flying was a whole new thing. We used the money that we'd been making to make touring a little more comfortable so we could tour longer and sound better every night.

...And Justice for All seemed to get a bad rap for its weak production, yet it was one of your most ambitious records. The lyrics seemed even angrier than anything to-date.

The lyrics were. I call that album the "complaining album." The production itself was the only thing that really bothered me. The songs were great; the lyrics were great...the production was not so great. The songs were a bit long and drawn out, but that's basically what we were into. It got a little too progressive, I think.

Lyrically, we were really into social things, watching CNN and the news all the time, and realizing that other people really do kinda control your life. The movie *...And Justice For All* turned our heads a bit. We discovered how much money influences certain things, and discovered how things work in the United States. How things might seem okay on the outside, but internally, they're corrupt.

On tour for that album you featured your only prop, the Lady Justice (aka "Doris") that would tumble down at the end of the show. Were you concerned about how it would look?

In the beginning, everyone is kinda scared about trying somethin' new. Especially if you're not sure it's gonna work, or you not sure if it's gonna look stupid (laughs), y'know? I couldn't tell if it was really fuckin' stupid, or really cool. It wasn't really in the middle, but you definitely noticed the damn thing. It was good to see the reaction on people's faces, when they saw the thing comin' down, or when the lights would be swinging. People weren't sure if that was supposed to happen or not! They'd be yelling at you, pointing, goin', "Hey, the lights are swingin'. Get out of the way!" I'd be up there laughing.

Doris's head was supposed to be on this rope: When the thing would fall, it would fall free, but it would have a rope so it could only go so far. Accidentally, the rope got loose and the head rolled down into the front row and over a security guard! Ha, ha!

Looking out into the audience must reveal some pretty strange things going on.

Oh, shit! I saw a guy in a wheelchair once, down in the front row. He was just getting crushed by people, but he didn't care. I'll see people crippled up or wearing casts in the front row, just sittin' there moshin' away. I can't remember where the hell it is, but every time we go there, I recognize this one fuckin' guy. He's got no hand on one arm. It's chopped at the wrist, so he puts his wrist in his mouth, so it looks like the whole hand is in his face, it's kinda sick looking!! I see that same guy every damn time! Also, chicks pull their tits out, all that shit.

You've taken some unique support bands on tour, like The Cult, Danzig, and Queensryche. Did you get along with the bands?

We did a two-week tour of the U.K. with Danzig, and one night we went out drinkin'. This guy wouldn't let us into his club, so we got pissed off. We went outside and knocked over some flower pots, then we seen some car. In the UK, they've got little, lightweight cars. And we decided that this one kinda had to get turned over (chuckles). We got on the side of this car, counted, rolled it over, and slowly walked away.

The next morning, I got a call from Bobby Schneider, who was our tour manager back then, saying, "What'd you guys do last night?" I told him, "Uh...we just went out drinkin'." He says, 'Do you know anything about a car turning over.' I said, "Uh, no."

Then he said, "Well, there's a policeman down here who wants to arrest you concerning a car that's been flipped over." So I figured I'd better go down and tell him (chuckles)! The car had been crushed in. The weight of the bottom had crushed in the top, so, I figured that car wasn't safe enough to drive anyway, ha ha! I saved the guy's life, maybe.

Touring with The Cult was strange. They were kinda cocky. Our crowd basically doesn't like any support act, especially in the States, and The Cult didn't really try hard to win the fans over or work with 'em. They basically took the attitude of, "Fuck you." It looked like they weren't having a good time at all, you know?

Queensryche were basically the opposite. It was difficult for them to be in front of our crowd, 'cause they're a bit lighter. They've gotten a little poppier over the years, they just aren't heavy metal. But they would come out every night and give 110 percent.

For the last show with The Cult, we got together and got some Ian Astbury wigs, and some hippy pants, and headbands, and put some pillows in our stomachs 'cause he was kinda fat back then. We went around onstage imitating him, and I don't think he really liked that at all; didn't really dig it.

There was this whole thing related to his girl on the road; her name was Renee. She was very strange; they were a strange couple, no doubt. We were playing out somewhere outdoors someplace, and I think there was a fair next door. Like any fair, you could go into the arcade area and win these nickel goldfish. She fell in love with this one gold fish, which they took on the bus. They'd call her "Edie," and put her in special water, and if it looked sick, they'd take it to the vet and spend a hundred bucks on this little fish that's worth maybe a nickel. She was infatuated by this fish: she'd put water in the microwave to heat for the fish! It was pretty bizarre.

Kirk's 24th birthday on stage in Japan, November 18, 1986.

At the end of the tour, we went to a pet store and got about 400 goldfish. We had 'em in these little catering trays, and we'd put towels under them, put water on them, and then put the goldfish in. So you could just pick the towel up, and the goldfish would stay in; the towel would act as a net. We were flipping these goldfish out on the stage! There were four hundred of them, flipping around! (chuckles) She didn't notice it right away, she thought they were little paper ones or somethin'. But they started flippin' around, and she FREAKED! She started collecting a few, trying to put 'em in her glass, and then she just snapped! She ran and locked herself in the bathroom (laughter). Everyone was running around stomping on them and shit. I remember Matt, who is now drummin' with Guns, was in the band, and I remember one landed on his snare drum, and he just picked it up and swallowed it (laughter)!

The last gig with Queensryche was pretty good. We had our "Justice" stuff set up behind theirs, so our scrim and a little walkway was above their stuff, so you could see what went on behind 'em on top of this little stage thing. During one of their songs, we hired about four male strippers, real gay lookin' guys, and they got up on our back amp line. Everyone could see 'em — the spotlights were right on them! But the band couldn't really see 'em, cause they were up so high behind 'em. These fags would be dancin' on the amps the whole time (laughs)! Queensryche didn't know what was goin' on.

Do most of the bands understand the humor behind the end of the tour prank sessions?

If a band doesn't really fuck with you at the end of the tour, you know it wasn't a good tour. You expect it, 'cause it's a fun thing, you know.

After your fourth album, you seemed to move into an era of "Awards Appearances," like the Grammies and MTV Awards.

"Damaged Justice" tour promotion.

It was a new thing for us. I remember our manager coming and saying, "They want you to play the Grammies." I thought, "Oh, man, I don't wanna fuckin' be a part of this crap." But then it was like, hey, this is an opportunity. You don't get to do this every day, a chance to get on national TV and show all these boring fucks what we're all about! So we kinda turned the whole thing around to our advantage, instead of kinda running away and hiding from it. It was the fans that put us there. They were the ones who were drawing all this attention, calling up MTV and saying, "Hey, where's the Metallica video?," and MTV not knowing who the fuck Metallica was. The underground word of mouth got around, and it was something that had to be reckoned with finally.

The first TV thing, which was the Grammies [February 22, 1989], really turned us off to TV. You can't do what you wanna do. It's all fuckin' planned out. Even though the Grammies are very hectic and there are millions of people running around, they basically told us, "You can't do this, you can't do that." In soundcheck, I remember we were playing the nice little beginning bit to "One," and then we kicked in to the double-bass "bra-ta-ta-ta-ta-ta-TA" —the machine gun fire—and they freaked out, and said, "Hold it! Stop! There's no way you can do this on TV."

Was it strange to look into the audience and see all those tuxedo-wearing musical bureaucrats?

No doubt! I mean, looking out there and seeing people's faces, and all these black and white tuxes. Everyone had rented their nice fuckin' suit, and were sittin' down there expecting some nice little awards show. It was like, 'Oh, we'll have a cocktail,' all this kinda crap. "Ahhhh, terrific, let's do lunch!," all that crap. Then we got up there and just started bashing away. They basically had to clap. I'm sure if they were sitting there by themselves, there's no way they would have clapped. They would have got up and left (laughter)!

The MTV thing was a lot looser and more fun. We could get away with a little more, 'cause it was a younger generation, you know. They understood why we were there. There were less limitations. That kinda helped us out with liking to do TV shows again. We went back on the Grammies a second time after that, and it was a lot more relaxed, too. We'd done it before, and knew what to expect.

You had a record release party at Madison Square Garden for the last album where 10,000 fans previewed Metallica; whose concept was that?

It was weird being there and not playing. I mean, the record played Madison Square Garden before we did, which is a pretty amazing fact. Lars and I were on our way to Europe for a promo tour, I think. It was my birthday, and we stuck around there doing interview crap and MTV drivel. Then we tried to see a reaction from people there. That was a risky thing to do, but a very unique idea.

It was actually the idea of some guy at Elektra, which is pretty amazing, that some record company guy would come up with that. They're really behind the band and want to try some different shit. We basically went with Elektra to begin with because they were a little bit more open-minded about things. When you're in a big venue like that, it's really hard to hear music. When you hear an album for the first time, you wanna be in your room, with the headphones on, or in a real personal kinda place. And this was out in the middle of everybody.

I was just waiting for "Nothing Else Matters" to come on, you know. To see if these people would just look at each other and throw up! (Laughter.) I was wondering how much peer pressure people were gonna put on each other; people going, "Do you like this?" "I dunno—do you like it?," looking at each other to see if they like it or not. People were really into it, which was pretty amazing.

It's ironic that a one time Venom fanatic like you would go on to write something as delicate as "Nothing Else Matters."

Yeah. It was pretty un-safe for us to do. That song just came about. That was never to be heard by anyone. It was my song, that I wrote and played in this hotel room and put it down on tape, never thinking it would surface with Metallica. Then the band heard it, and liked it, and it grew from there.

I basically remember Bob Rock saying, "Are you sure you want to sing this song like this?" (Laughter.) I'd say, "Yeah, man, 'cause this is how it was fuckin' meant to be!" I didn't really want it to be a big song, you know. Because the way it was written was with one guitar and one voice, and that's it. I still dig the demo a lot better [than the LP version]. But then again, there's so much you can do with it, that you don't want to NOT try the stuff, like putting the orchestration in. I loved that.

"Don't Tread on Me" really raised the hackles of some conservative critics, who felt it was politically incorrect during the invasion of Kuwait. That must have really steamed you.

They basically took their own opinions, and put 'em in there, concerning the song. They thought the song was cashing in on the Saddam thing, and the mid-East crisis. It had nothing to do with that really. The song was about one of the first military flags, the Culpepper Minutemen's Gaston flag.

People love to point the finger, and go, "That's wrong!" or "That's not socially correct now! Oh, that's not good for our kids! That's not good for the ozone! Don't do that!" All this "don't do" kinda shit! (Laughter.) It's fuckin' amazing that people could just sit there and write down what they thought, and basically fuck up a review like that! It made them look like such assholes, for them to bring their own personal views into the thing. Who wants to read that shit? No one does, except themselves. People just dig in to find something wrong. They'd rather waste their time findin' somethin' wrong than findin' the good parts about it—they'll push them out of the way just to find the shit.

That's pretty much the way the PMRC worked. They'd look for bad shit and find it. 'Cause you're gonna find what you're lookin' for, even if it ain't there to someone else. Or ain't there at all!

What was your general impression of the Guns N' Roses/Metallica tour they said could never happen?

It disappointed me a lot that a certain someone [presumably Guns' frontman Axl Rose] didn't compromise too well. It was difficult to get what we wanted. It really sucked, because we'd have a bargaining point, but then, he'd say, "Forget it. It ain't gonna happen!" He'd pull that fuckin' childish shit. That's not the way you do business. It was pretty difficult. But overall, it was good for us, I think. We did snatch a lot of Guns fans by the neck, and kinda showed 'em what this was all about. I guess they thought Guns N' Roses were the heaviest thing on the planet, and they fuckin' found out wrong.

The tour took a strange turn when you were burned by a flashpot during a show in Montreal. How did it happen? (Following the incident, old guitar roadie and Metal Church guitarist John Marshall filled in as rhythm guitar, while James sang, in an arrangement strangely similar to his post-skateboarding accident stint with Ozzy in 1986.)

I was standing in the wrong place. There was a little miscommunication before the show. The pyro man would come in and if something was different, he would come in and say, "This is going to be different. I'm going to...," So basically, the "Fade to Black" pyro was gonna be out on the wings, and he told me not to go out there. But he neglected to tell me, or I didn't understand quite well enough, it was there, as well as the old pyro. The way that it worked was that the pyro was underneath a grillwork, and you couldn't really see it. So I didn't know what was goin' on. Basically, it fuckin' went off right under me. It could've been a lot worse.

Being a frontman [without playing rhythm guitar] was weird. It reminded me how much I really loved fuckin' playing rhythm guitar. In a way it was pretty cool, 'cause I could do a lot of things with my hands, and I wasn't so tied down to certain monitors I'd ordinarily have to stand under. You could basically go anywhere. You didn't have to lug a guitar around. There were other points, though, where I'd go, "Fuck—now I'm gonna have to stand here. What the fuck do I do, now that I don't have a guitar to play?" Especially during some of the older songs, where there's a lot of guitar work or instrumental shit. It's like, "What the fuck do I do?" I'd just leave. Go backstage and have a beer (chuckles). They were the ones who were drawing all this attention.

People were real into it, which was pretty amazing.

METALLI-MERCHANDISE

AT THE DAWN of the 1980's, adolescent metal-lovers were literally marked by a common brand: wherever they might be hanging out at any given moment—browsing through record stores in suburban shopping malls, loitering in front of popular music clubs waiting for a weekend gig, haunting homefronts and parks with their boom-boxes blasting in all directions—their teen torsos were adorned by the ghoulish, skeletal creations of Derek Riggs.

Riggs, as every self-respecting metal afficionado knows, was the Iron Maiden sleeve artist, whose brilliant marketing creation, the gore-soaked Maiden mascot Eddie The Head, assumed the universal familiarity of the Rick Griffin/Stanley Mouse-penned skull designs that so effectively identified the Grateful Dead and that band's legions of Deadhead followers. What was it about the skull, that unmistakable symbol of doom and decay, that drew such a hypnotic response from T-shirt buyers the world over?

The Iron Maiden designs that dominated the market through the mid-1980's would become less visible as the band's popularity waned and a new band and artist captured the limelight: Metallica and their talented pen-man, Pushead.

Pushead (whose real name is Brian Schroeder) began his affiliation with Metallica after meeting James Hetfield

---

Opposite: James with Zorlac "Metallica" skateboards.

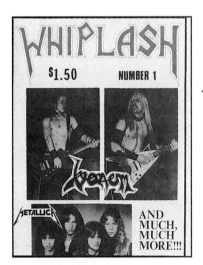

Two of the most influential and collectable early fanzines: Aaardschok and Whiplash.

during a 1984 Venom gig at San Francisco's Kabuki Theater. James, who was familiar with the aspiring artist's work before, requested some Pushead-designed shirts, which featured an assortment of pre-Metallica imagery. Soon after receiving the shirts, the frontman contacted Pushead again—this time with an idea for a sleeve design.

The concept materialized on Metallica's 1986 "Damage, Inc." tour shirt. With their arresting image of a skull impaled by two spiked clubs, the shirts sold by the truckload, further popularizing the skeletal imagery that had become a taken-for-granted staple of all metal merchandise.

"Now, while people have been saying that they want to get away from the skull thing," the popular artist told a journalist in 1991, "they still want at least one token skull shirt in their merchandise lineup, 'cause they know kids will buy it."

Despite the fact that everyone appears to have jumped on the skull bandwagon, punters will most likely be moved to purchase only the most distinctive representations at gig merchandise stands. "It seems like in metal, you really do need an identity," says Pushead. "Especially with so much stuff out there."

The busy art-man maintains a high profile, with over a dozen Metallica T-shirt designs to his credit. His bare-boned creations include one which, with a battered, bloodied stump swinging from a parachute, incorporates the battle-scarred theme of ...*And Justice for All*'s "One"; another which became the 1991 Metallica tour logo, depicts one skull holding another in contemplative, Hamlet fashion. The macabre Pushead signature art even adorns video boxes and skateboards, not to mention the sleeves of other bands like Rush, Motley Crue, Aerosmith, Prong, Corrosion of Conformity, and Hirax. Pushead also markets a separate merchandise collection not associated with his rock ventures called the Kuro line.

Life on the Metallica merchandise front doesn't begin and end with Pushead-related items, however. Earlier T-shirts like Metallica's first, which simply displayed their logo alongside the phrase "The Young Metal Attack," are far rarer catches. A second band shirt, featuring their trademark logo and the now-legendary "Metal up Your Ass" slogan, as well as the official shirt from the "Kill 'em all for One" tour of 1983, are vintage Metallica trophies.

Other silkscreened treasures would enhance any Metallishrine. Mark DeVito, an Oakland shirt designer, entered a 1988 display contest which required entrants to come up with a concept for advertising a string of upcoming Metallica shows. DeVito and a

friend built a six foot display that depicted the four band members staring out from a Cap'n Crunch cereal box, with the logo cleverly changed to read "Cap'ns of Krunch." Lars Ulrich got wind of DeVito's ambitious design and asked for a scaled-down model of the display. "I made the model and also gave him a xeroxed layout of the design," says DeVito. "I had forgotten about the whole thing when, three months later, Jason debuted the design on a T-shirt at the 1990 Grammys. They had made similar shirts for their crew, and had even used the design on European and American tour laminates. I was blown away."

Other DeVito merchandise designs, many of which ended up on subsequent crew shirts, include "Trails We Have Crept" (based

Berkeley artist Mark Devito with samples of his work.

on the "Tales From the Crypt" comic-book logo), "Yosemite Slam" (inspired by Warner Bros.' Yosemite Sam cartoon character), "Harvester of Sapporo/Damaged Liver Tour" (which borrows from Pushead's "Damaged Justice" tour design but adds a few humorous modifications), and a "Griffinized" Grateful Dead-inspired Metallica logo (Rick Griffin drew poster art for The Dead until his tragic death via a motorcycle accident on August 17, 1991). "When I showed this logo to Lars," laughs DeVito, "he said that one would have to be on acid to read it." The wise-cracking drummer signed "Where's the acid?" on a copy he autographed for Mark.

Demos and bootlegs also add a nice touch to the collector's mantel. The "must have" tapes are "No Life 'til Leather" (1982), essentially a demo tape of most of the songs from the first Metallica record, and "Live Metal up Your Ass" (11/29/82). There are original, Hetfield-stenciled sleeves that go with both of these tapes, but they're near-impossible to find. Other indispensable demos include "Whiplash"/"No Remorse" (2/83), "Fight Fire with Fire"/"Ride the Lightning"/"When Hell Freezes Over" (the original title of "Call of Ktulu")/"Creeping Death" (12/83), and the band's original "Metal Massacre" demo (1981), which included practice versions of two NWOBHM cover songs, "Let It Loose" and "Killing Time," in addition to Metallica's first song "Hit the Lights."

Demos featuring Cliff Burton and Kirk Hammett from their pre-Metallica days are also floating around. Burton can be heard on "Such a Shame" (1982), with early band Trauma, while Hammett appears on a 1982 Exodus demo featuring such Kirk-penned tunes as "Death and Domination," "Whipping Queen," and "Warlords." (Plenty of early live Exodus bootlegs abound as well, which feature such amazing Hammett compositions as "Hellsbreath" and "Impaler".)

Unauthorized vinyl bootlegs are available on such unauthorized (and often-times nonexistent) "labels" as After Hours, Bongwater, Hellaslam, and Metal Message. As many as 500 bootlegs have been reported, with such outrageous titles as *Fucking Nuts, We'll Nail You Down, Acting Like a Maniac,* and *Time for Some Fucking Danish Beer,* etc., etc., etc. Especially noteworthy are the many Cliff Burton "memorial" bootlegs such as *The Final Gig* and *The Freak's Not Here.* While unauthorized records often boast rare performances and

Above: Yosemite Slam. Below: Original sleeves for "No Life 'til Leather" and "Live Metal up Your Ass" demos.

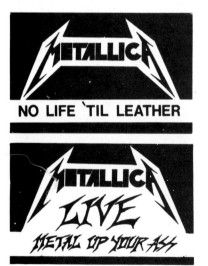

impressive outside packaging, beware of sub-standard sound quality and even the wrong band's music showing up on the platter within. Song titles are often (intentionally) misspelled (e.g. "Sanitation" rather than "Sanitarium") for comic relief.

Metallica's massive authorized vinyl output can leave the collector breathless and intimidated. Oftentimes, the release of a mere single can spark a harried hunt for what seems like a zillion different versions of the disc. The "Creeping Death" 12-inch EP (*Music for Nations*, 1985) is a good example of this syndrome: it was released in black, blue, green, clear, gold, and mixed-vinyl versions. Meanwhile, special-edition gatefold edition albums, white-label promo copies, and freaky, one-of-a-kind limited pressings pose similar collecting nightmares.

Personal favorites? A French pressing of *Ride the Lightning* (1985) with, thanks to a printing error, a green cover (as opposed to the customary blue); the first Megaforce pressing of *Ride the Lightning* (1985), in which "For Whom the Bell Tolls" is accidently written on the sleeve as "For Whom the Bells Toll"; a glow-in-the-dark "Fade to Black" 12-inch promo single (Elektra, 1985); and a "Master of Puppets" French 7-inch promo (*Music for Nations*/N.E.W., 1986), that comes with its own cover sleeve.

The list goes on. There are those readily accessible items like the *Cliff 'em All*, *2 Of One*, and *"A Year and a Half in the Life of Metallica"* videos, not to mention the Brockum-marketed stable of tour merchandise mementos including pins, badges, tour books, sweat pants, tank-tops, hats, patches–everything but the proverbial kitchen Metallisink. There's the Metallica painter's can that comes with a compilation set; Elektra-issued items such as a marble paperweight, a plastic dagger, and a snake-in-a-bag promotional souvenir.

Unfortunately, the above hardly skims the surface of what is available to the persistent Metallica merchandise hunter. And Metalli-junkies the world over will take no solace from the fact that there's *much more to come*. Metallica cereal prizes? Action figures? Illustrated fast-food cups? "Alcoholica" approved-and-patented beer bongs? Only time will tell....

Cap'ns of Krunch design which adorned crew shirts and laminates for "Damaged Justice" tour.

A COMPLETE METALLICA DISCOGRAPHY

SEVEN-INCH SINGLES	LABEL	ISSUE/DATE
Master of Puppets/Sanitarium	Music For Nations 11575	France /1986
One/The Prince	Elektra 7-69329	U.S./1988
One/One [white label promo]	Elektra 7-69329	U.S./1988
One [promo-only / PS]		Japan
Eye of the Beholder/Breadfan	Elektra 7-69357	U.S./1988
Eye of the Beholder/Eye of the Beholder [white label promo]	Elektra 7-69357	U.S./1988
One/Seek and Destroy [live/first issue w/poster]	Vertigo METAL 5	U.K.
One/One [Radio edit/promo-only PS 45 w/history of song]	Vertigo METDJ 5	U.K.
Harvester of Sorrow/Harvester of Sorrow [promo-only/PS white cover w/Harvester Of Sorrow written on it]	Vertigo METDJ 2	U.K.
Enter Sandman/Stone Cold Crazy	Vertigo METAL 7	U.K.
Enter Sandman/Stone Cold Crazy [picture disc]	Vertigo METAL 7	U.K.
The Unforgiven/Killing Time	Vertigo METAL 8	U.K.
The Unforgiven/Killing Time/The Unforgiven [demo, w/insert]	Vertigo METAL 812	U.K.
Nothing Else Matters/Enter Sandman (live)	Vertigo METAL 10	U.K.
The Unforgiven [promo-only]	Vertigo METDJ 8	U.K.
Wherever I May Roam/Fade to Black (live)	Vertigo METAL9	U.K./1992
Sad But True/Nothing Else Matters	Vertigo METAL11	U.K./1993

12-INCH SINGLES	LABEL	ISSUE/DATE
Whiplash (remix)/Seek and Destroy/Phantom Lord (live...?)	Megaforce MRS-04	U.S./1984
For Whom the Bell Tolls [white label promo]	Elektra ED 5026	U.S./1984
Fade to Black [white label promo on green wax]	Elektra ED 5042	U.S./1984
Jump in the Fire/Phantom Lord (live)/Seek and Destroy (live)	Music For Nations 12KUT105	U.K./ 1984
Jump in the Fire/Phantom Lord (live)/Seek and Destroy (live) [red wax]	Music For Nations CV12KUT105	U.K./1984
Creeping Death/Am I Evil/Blitzkrieg [released in seven diff. colors: red, blue, black, clear, green, white, and gold/no cover]	Music For Nations 12KUT112	U.K./1984
Fade to Black [white label promo]	Elektra ED 5044	U.S./1984
Master of Puppets [white label promo edit]	Elektra ED 5139	U.S./1986
The $5.98 EP Garage Days Re-Revisited [white label promo+ reg. label/out of print]	Elektra 9 60257-1	U.S./1987
The $5.98 EP Garage Days Re-Revisited [without The Wait/out of print]	Vertigo METAL 112	U.K./1987
Eye of the Beholder [white label promo edit]	Elektra ED 5332	U.S./1988
One [white label promo edit]	Elektra ED 5349	U.S./1988
...And Justice for All [white label promo edit]	Elektra ED 5396	U.S./1988
Eye of the Beholder [promo w/special cover: same as U.S. 7-inch]	Vertigo AJFA 112	U.K./1988
Harvester of Sorrow/Breadfan/The Prince	Vertigo METAL 212	U.K. /1988
Harvester of Sorrow/Breadfan/The Prince [promo w/white cover labelled Harvester of Sorrow]	Vertigo METAL 212	U.K./1988
Harvester of Sorrow/Breadfan/The Prince [promo w/white cover labelled ...And Justice for All/ Metallipromo]	Vertigo METDJ 212	U.K./1988
One/For Whom the Bell Tolls/Welcome Home (Sanitarium) [last two live]	Vertigo METAL 512	U.K./1989
One [promo white cover w/Pushead drawing]	Vertigo METDJ 512	U.K./1989
One (demo)/For Whom the Bell Tolls/Creeping Death [special gatefold/last two live]	Vertigo METG 512	U.K./1989

The Good The Bad & The Live	Vertigo METAL 612	U.K./1990
[6 1/2 Year Anniversary 12" Collection w/Jump in the Fire,		
Creeping Death, $5.98 EP, Harvester of Sorrow, One,		
Special 6 1/2 Year Live EP/comes in special box w/poster]		
Jump in the Fire/Seek and Destroy (live)/Phantom Lord (live)	Vertigo METAL 312	U.K./1990
Creeping Death/Am I Evil/Blitzkrieg [reissue]	Vertigo METAL 412	U.K./1990
Creeping Death/Jump in the Fire [reissue]	Vertigo LP 842-219-1	U.K./1990
Enter Sandman/Holier Than Thou (demo)/	Vertigo METAL 712	U.K./1991
Stone Cold Crazy/Enter Sandman (demo)		
Enter Sandman [promo only]	Vertigo METDJ 712	U.K./1991
Enter Sandman/Holier Than Thou (demo)/	Vertigo METBX 712	U.K./1991
Stone Cold Crazy/Enter Sandman (demo) [box w/4 prints]		
The Unforgiven/Killing Time/So What/The Unforgiven (demo)	Vertigo METAL 812	U.K./1992
The Unforgiven/Of Wolf and Man [promo only]	Vertigo METDJ 812	U.K./1992
Nothing Else Matters/Enter Sandman (live)/		
Harvester of Sorrow (live)/Nothing Else Matters (demo)	Vertigo METAL 1012	U.K./1992
Wherever I May Roam/Medley: Last Caress,		
Am I Evil, Battery (live)/Wherever I May Roam (demo)	Vertigo METAL 912	U.K./1992
Sad But True/Nothing Else Matters/Creeping Death (live)/		
Sad But True (demo)	Vertigo METAL 1112	U.K./1993

ALBUMS	**LABEL**	**ISSUE/DATE**
Kill 'em All	Megaforce MRI 069	U.S./1983
Kill 'em All	Elektra 9 60766-1	U.S./1988
[reissue w/2 bonus tracks: Am I Evil and Blitzkrieg]		
Kill 'em All	Music For Nations MFN 7 DM	U.K./1983
[direct metal mastered double LP; gatefold w/poster]		
Ride the Lightning	Megaforce MRI 769	U.S./1984
Ride the Lightning	Elektra 9 60396-1	U.S./1984
Ride the Lightning [white label promo]	Elektra 9 60396-1	U.S./1984
Ride the Lightning [direct metal mastered double-LP; gatefold]	Music For Nations MFN 27 DM	U.K./1984
Ride the Lightning [cover green, not blue]		France 1984
Master of Puppets	Elektra 9 60439-1	U.S./1986
Master of Puppets	Elektra 9 60439-1	U.S./1986
[white label promo w/warning label		
re: the '"F" word on "Damage, Inc."]		
Master of Puppets	Music For Nations MFN 60	U.K./1986
Master of Puppets	Music For Nations MFN 60 DM	U.K./1987
[direct metal mastered double LP; gatefold w/poster]		
...And Justice for All	Elektra 9 60812-1	U.S./1988
...And Justice for All [w/promo labels]	Elektra 9 60812-1	U.S./1988
...And Justice for All [w/bonus track The Prince]	Sony/CBS 25 AP 5178/9	Japan/1988
...And Justice for All	Vertigo VERH 61	U.K./1988
Metallica	Elektra 9 61113-1	U.S./1991
Metallica	Vertigo 5 10022-1	U.K./1991

PICTURE DISCS (10- & 12-INCH) & SHAPED DISCS	**LABEL**	**ISSUE/DATE**
Kill 'em All [title painted in red]	Megaforce	U.S.
Whiplash	Megaforce MRS-04	U.S./1987
Kill 'em All [title painted in blue]	Music For Nations MFN 7P	U.K./1986
Ride the Lightning	Music For Nations MF 27P	U.K./1986
Master of Puppets	Music For Nations MFN 60P	U.K./1986
Creeping Death/Am I Evil/Blitzkrieg	Music For Nations P12 KUT	U.K./1984
Jump in the Fire/Seek and Destroy (live)/Phantom Lord (live)	Music For Nations PKUT	U.K./1986
[shaped]		
Jump in the Fire [uncut pic disc]	Music For Nations RKUT	U.K./1986
One/Seek and Destroy (live)	Vertigo METPD 50	U.K./1988
[10-inch pic disc comes w/cardboard back, printed w/lyrics]		

CD's	LABEL	ISSUE/DATE
Kill 'em All	Megaforce MRI 069	U.S.
Kill 'em All [w/two bonus tracks: Am I Evil and Blitzkrieg]	Elektra 960766-2	U.S.
Kill 'em All [w/out abovementioned bonus tracks, which were deleted by Elektra in late 1992]	Elektra 960766-2	U.S.
Ride the Lightning	Elektra 9 60396-2	U.S.
Master of Puppets	Elektra 9 60439-2	U.S.
The $9.98 CD Garage Days Re-Revisited [out of print]	Elektra 9 60757-2	U.S.
...And Justice for All	Elektra 9 60812-2	U.S.
Mandatory Metallica [seven-song compilation; promo only]	Elektra PR 8071-2	U.S.
Mandatory Metallica [same as other, but w/edited version of "One"]	Elektra PR8071-2	U.S.
Eye of the Beholder (Edit) [promo-only]	Elektra PR 8028-2	U.S.
One (Edit)/One (LP) [promo-only]	Elektra PR 8044-2	U.S.
...And Justice for All (Edit + LP version) [promo-only; green disc]	Elektra PR 8099-2	U.S.
Master Of Puppets	Music For Nations CDMFN 60	U.K.
Ride the Lightning	Music For Nations CDMFN 27	U.K.
Kill 'em All	Music For Nations CDMFN 7	U.K.
Harvester of Sorrow/Breadfan/The Prince	Vertigo METCD 2	U.K.
One/For Whom the Bell Tolls (live)/ Welcome Home (Sanitarium) (live)	Vertigo METCD 5	U.K.
Whiplash/Ride the Lightning/ Welcome Home (Sanitarium)/One [promo-only]	Vertigo METCD 100	U.K.
One/The Prince [three inch]	Elektra 9 69329-9	U.K.
..And Justice for All [w/bonus track The Prince]	CBS/Sony 39DP 5176	Japan
One/Breadfan/For Whom the Bell/Tolls/ Welcome Home (Sanitarium) (live)/One (demo)	CBS/Sony 23DP 5438	Japan
One Breadfan [3-inch]	CBS/Sony 10EP 3077	Japan
Stone Cold Crazy [promo-only]	Elektra PRCD 8224-2	U.S.
Enter Sandman Stone Cold Crazy [3-inch single]	CBS/Sony SRDS 8204	Japan
Enter Sandman [box w/4 drawers]	Vertigo METCD 7	U.K.
Enter Sandman [promo-only]	Elektra PRCD 8407-2	U.S.
Enter Sandman (edit)	Elektra PRCD 8421-2	U.S.
Enter Sandman/Stone Cold Crazy/Enter Sandman (demo)	Vertigo 868733-2	Germany
The Unforgiven/Killing Time [3-inch single]	CBS/Sony SRDS 8214	Japan
The Unforgiven [promo only]	Elektra PRCD 8478-2	U.S.
The Unforgiven [promo-edit]	Elektra PRCD 8479-2	U.S.
The Unforgiven/Killing Time/The Unforgiven (demo)	Vertigo METCD 8	U.K.
The Unforgiven/Killing Time/The Unforgiven (demo) [w/poster]	Vertigo	Australia
Nothing Else Matters/Enter Sandman (live)/ Harvester of Sorrow (live)/Nothing Else Matters (demo)	Vertigo METCD 10	U.K.
Nothing Else Matters [promo-only]	Elektra PRCD 8530-2	U.S.
Nothing Else Matters/Enter Sandman (live) [3-inch single]	CBS/Sony	Japan
Nothing Else Matters (edit)	Elektra PRCD 8531-2	U.S.
Live at Wembley w/Enter Sandman (live)/ Sad But True (live)/Nothing Else Matters (live)	Vertigo METCL 10	U.K.
Wherever I May Roam [promo-only]	Elektra PRCD 8591-2	U.S.
Sad But True/So What/Harvester of Sorrow (live)	Vertigo 864 411-2	Australia/1992
Wherever I May Roam (edit)[promo only]	Elektra PRCD 8592-2	U.S./1992
Wherever I May Roam/Fade to Black (live)/ Wherever I May Roam (demo)	Vertigo METCD 9	U.K./1992
Wherever I May Roam/Medley: Last Caress, Am I Evil, Battery (live)	Vertigo METCB 9	U.K./1992
Sad But True [promo only]	Elektra PRCD 8646-2	U.S./1992
Sad But True/Nothing Else Matters (Elevator Version)/ Creeping Death (live)/Sad But True (demo)	Vertigo METCD 11	U.K./1993
Sad But True/Nothing Else Matters (live)/ Sad But True (demo)	Vertigo METCH 11	U.K./1993
Wherever I May Roam/Fade to Black (live)/ Medley: Last Caress, Am I Evil, Battery (live)	Sony 6633	Japan/1993